Minoo Moallem offers a fascinating discussion of the Persian carpet as a site of identity, aesthetic object, and modern commodity. In a genealogical account that traces the history of Persian carpets as imperial and civilizational objects in the mid-nineteenth century to national and diasporic commodities today, she insightfully explores the affective experiences and material conditions that undergird the history of their production and consumption.

Ali Behdad, Professor and John Charles Hillis Chair, Literature, University of California, Los Angeles and author of *Camera Orientalis: Reflections on Photography of the Middle East*

I admire the rare convergence in Minoo Moallem's *Persian Carpets* of questions of political economy, materialist history, and the aesthetic and sensuous lives of commodities. The book promises to be essential reading for feminist scholars of connoisseurship and consumer capitalism in the making of empire.

Parama Roy, Professor, English, University of California, Davis

In this eye-opening journey, Minoo Moallem offers an astute genealogical reading of the shifting production, consumption, and representation of the Persian carpet from the imperial era to the present. Her perceptive analysis reveals how an object of exotic Orientalia was transformed into a national identity-marker, only to subsequently turn into a home-making icon for a diasporic community. Transcending multiple binarisms – East/West, tradition/ modernity, nation/diaspora – the book is an illuminating study of transnational interconnectivities shaped within and across borders.

Ella Shohat, Professor, Middle Eastern and Islamic Studies, New York University, and author of *Taboo Memories, Diasporic Voices*

Persian Carpets redirects the magic flight of Orientalist fantasies into Iranian village workshops, commercial factories, merchant bazaars, African mosques, connoisseurs' vaults, world fair pavilions, museum displays, cinema screens, Internet auction sites as well as homes – both modest and ostentatious – blessed by their woven beauty around the world. With a keen sense of the carpet as art, craft, commodity, and cultural icon, Moallem sheds light on the role carpets play in defining gender, class, religion, ethnicity and nation as well as transnational identities in diaspora. A model of interdisciplinary inquiry, this book speaks to scholars as well as general readers interested in taking a fresh look at the carpets under their feet.

Gina Marchetti, Professor, Comparative Literature, University of Hong Kong

This marvelous book is a welcome contribution to the literature on cultural commodification, to recent debates on affect and materiality, and to classic debates on Orientalism, spectacle and labor. It is also a highly original effort to link the problems of diasporic subjectivity to the subject of the trade in long-distance luxury goods. It will be of great interest to anthropologists and cultural historians as well as to scholars concerned with the sublime dimensions of global commodity chains.

Arjun Appadurai, Paulette Goddard Professor, Media, Culture, and Communication, New York University

PERSIAN CARPETS

Persian Carpets: The Nation as a Transnational Commodity tracks the Persian carpet as an exotic and mythological object, as a commodity, and as an image from mid-nineteenth-century England to contemporary Iran and the Iranian diaspora. Following the journey of this single object, the book brings issues of labor into conversation with the politics of aesthetics. It focuses on the carpet as a commodity that crosses the boundaries of private and public, religious and secular, culture and economy, modern and traditional, home and diaspora, and art and commodity to tell the story of transnational interconnectivity.

Bringing transnational feminist cultural studies, ethnography, and network studies within the same frame of reference, this book sheds light on Orientalia as civilizational objects that emerged as commodities in the encounter between the West and the many directly or indirectly colonized Middle Eastern and West Asian cultures, focusing on the specific example of Persian carpets as some of the most extensively valued and traded objects since colonial modernity.

Minoo Moallem is Professor of Gender and Women's Studies at the University of California at Berkeley.

The Routledge Series for Creative Teaching and Learning in Anthropology
Editor: Richard H. Robbins, SUNY Plattsburgh, and
Luis A. Vivanco, University of Vermont

This series is dedicated to innovative, unconventional ways to connect under-graduate students and their lived concerns about our social world to the power of social science ideas and evidence. We seek to publish titles that use anthropology to help students understand how they benefit from exposing their own lives and activities to the power of anthropological thought and analysis. Our goal is to help spark social science imaginations and, in doing so, open new avenues for meaningful thought and action.

Books in this series pose questions and problems that speak to the complexities and dynamism of modern life, connecting cutting edge research in exciting and relevant topical areas with creative pedagogy.

Available

The Baseball Glove
History, Material, Meaning, and Value
David Jenemann

Persian Carpets
The Nation as a Transnational Commodity
Minoo Moallem

Forthcoming

Seafood
From Ocean to Plate
Richard Wilk & Shingo Hamada

Love Letters
Saving Romance in the Digital Age
Michelle Janning

For a full list of titles in this series, please visit www.routledge.com

PERSIAN CARPETS

The Nation as a Transnational Commodity

Minoo Moallem

Routledge
Taylor & Francis Group

NEW YORK AND LONDON

First published 2018
by Routledge
711 Third Avenue, New York, NY 10017

and by Routledge
2 Park Square, Milton Park, Abingdon, Oxon, OX14 4RN

Routledge is an imprint of the Taylor & Francis Group, an informa business

Library of Congress Cataloging-in-Publication Data
Names: Moallem, Minoo, author.
Title: Persian carpets : the nation as a transnational commodity / Minoo Moallem.
Description: New York, NY : Routledge, 2018. | Series: The Routledge series for creative teaching and learning in anthropology | Includes bibliographical references and index. | Description based on print version record and CIP data provided by publisher; resource not viewed.
Identifiers: LCCN 2017061062 (print) | LCCN 2018011316 (ebook) | ISBN 9781315266435 (Master Ebook) | ISBN 9781351970099 (Web pdf) | ISBN 9781351970075 (Mobipocket) | ISBN 9781351970082 (ePub) | ISBN 9781138290242 | ISBN 9781138290242q(hardback :alk. paper) | ISBN 9781138290259(pbk. :alk. paper) | ISBN 9781315266435(ebk)
Subjects: LCSH: Rugs, Persian. | Carpets—Iran. | Orientalism.
Classification: LCC NK2809.P4 (ebook) | LCC NK2809.P4 M63 2018 (print) | DDC 746.7/55—dc23
LC record available at https://lccn.loc.gov/2017061062

ISBN: 978-1-138-29024-2 (hbk)
ISBN: 978-1-138-29025-9 (pbk)
ISBN: 978-1-315-26643-5 (ebk)

Typeset in New Baskerville
by Apex CoVantage, LLC

CONTENTS

SERIES FOREWORD

The premise of these short books on the *Anthropology of Stuff* is that stuff talks, that written into the biographies of everyday items of our lives—coffee, T-shirts, computers, iPods, flowers, drugs, and so forth—are the stories that make us who we are and that make the world the way it is. From their beginnings, each item bears the signature of the people who extracted, manufactured, picked, caught, assembled, packaged, delivered, purchased, and disposed of it. And in our modern market-driven societies, our lives are dominated by the pursuit of stuff.

Examining stuff is also an excellent way to teach and learn about what is exciting and insightful about anthropological and sociological ways of knowing. Students, as with virtually all of us, can relate to stuff, while at the same time discovering through these books that it can provide new and fascinating ways of looking at the world.

Stuff, or commodities and things, are central, of course, to all societies, to one extent or another. Whether it is yams, necklaces, horses, cattle, or shells, the acquisition, accumulation, and exchange of things is central to the identities and relationships that tie people together and drive their behavior. But never, before now, has the craving for stuff reached the level it has; and never before have so many people been trying to convince each other that acquiring more stuff is what they most want to do. As a consequence, the creation, consumption, and disposal of stuff now threaten the planet itself. Yet to stop or even slow down the manufacture and accumulation of stuff would threaten the viability of our economy, on which our society is built.

This raises various questions. For example, what impact does the compulsion to acquire stuff have on our economic, social, and political well-being, as well as on our environment? How do we come to believe that there are certain things that we must have? How do we come to value some commodities or form of commodities above others? How have we managed to create commodity chains that link peasant farmers in Colombia or gold miners in Angola to wealthy residents of New York or teenagers in Nebraska? Who comes up with the ideas for stuff and how do they translate those ideas into things for people to buy? Why do we sometimes consume stuff that is not very good for us? These short books examine such questions, and more.

ACKNOWLEDGEMENTS

As a feminist scholar of postcolonial studies with a profound commitment to bringing into conversation questions of political economy with cultural studies, this project has provided me a fantastic opportunity to think deeply about this connection through a tangible and material commodity such as the Persian carpet. Moving from mostly subject-centered scholarship to the world of objects and commodities as a site of research, this book has pushed me to leave my academic comfort zone and to explore new and unfamiliar fields of knowledge production. Such a scholarly move could not happen without the institutional and collegial support I was fortunate to have during various stages of this project.

I wish to thank Richard Robbins for his interest in this work for its inclusion in the Routledge *Anthropology of Stuff* book series. I am also grateful to Samantha Barbaro and Erik Zimmerman and the editorial team at Routledge for their help and support in various stages of this project. My special thanks to Parama Roy and two other anonymous reviewers from Routledge for their careful review and helpful comments. Anitra Griselda provided me with brilliant editorial insights. My superb research assistants Nina Torabzadeh and Midori Chen helped me with the bibliography and copyrights permissions. Sahar Namazikhah assisted me with collecting some archival information. I visited many carpet archives and libraries, including Kidderminster Carpet Museum Archive, Bodleian Library, Bibiothéque Nationale de la France, History of Advertising Trust, The National Art Library and The National Archives in London; Médiathèque du musée du quai Branly in Paris, Textile Museum in DC, Textile Museum of Lyon, Institut du Monde Arabe, Rasam Arabzadeh Museum, and Tehran Carpet Museum. I thank the librarians and archivists for their assistance. I am also grateful to Baku- based media and textile artist Faig Ahmed for his permission to use the image of one of his deconstructed carpets as the cover of this book. I would not have been able to complete this project without the funding support I received from UC Berkeley, including the Abigail Reynolds Hodgen Fund and Al-Fallah Award.

I was invited to present parts of this manuscript as a keynote or featured speaker at programs and events that included the Center for Middle Eastern Studies at UC Berkeley; Gender and Women's Studies and Iranian Studies at UC Irvine; Department of Gender and Women at the University of Illinois at Urbana–Champaign; Transnational Cinema Conference in NYU Abu Dhabi; Center for Race and Gender at UC Berkeley; Women, Gender, and Sexuality Studies at Trinity College; Global Studies at Duke University; Moving, Mobility, and Belonging Conference at the University of British Columbia; the Legacy of Materialist Feminist Conference at Princeton; the Society for Multi-Ethnic Studies in Europe; Institute for Research on Women at Rutgers University; Women and Gender Studies at Arizona State; and the San Jose Tech Museum. I am indebted to the organizers and audiences for their interest and engagement with this project.

I started to work on this project more than a decade ago. I received a fellowship from USC to create a digital project entitled "Nation on the Move," designed by Erik Loyer in an issue edited by Tara McPherson and Steve Anderson in *Vectors. Journal of Culture and Technology in a Dynamic Vernacular* 2:2 (October 2007). Some of the ideas in this book were first explored in the context of that digital project, even though I have significantly developed them in this book. Also, a version of Chapter 1 was published in Radha Hedge, ed., *Circuits of Visibility. Gender and Transnational Media Cultures* (New York University Press, 2011).

I also wish to thank Caren Kaplan, Inderpal Grewal, Ella Shohat, Parama Roy, and Robyn Weigman for their friendship and encouragement from the beginning of this project. I am also appreciative for the support of many friends and colleagues, including Tara McPherson, Sima Shakhsari, Laura Wexler, Danielle Juteau, Mimi T. Nguyen, Gina Marchetti, Deniz Gokturk, Deborah Cohler, Ali Behdad, Suad Joseph, Behrooz Ghamari Tabrizi, Nasrin Rahimieh, Eric Smoodin, Soraya Tlatli, Jennifer Terry, Laura Kang, Robert Corber, Marisol de Cadena, Emily Gottreich, Radha Hedge, Tani Barlow, Catherine Ceniza Choy, Robert Stam, Bharat Trehan, Brita Sands, Lisa Bloom, Roddey Reid, Natasha Lee, Madeleine Dobie, Miriam Cook, Robert Dun, Naomi Schneider, Ann Martin, Mahmoud Boddoohi, Alfred Jessel, Khosrow Ninijani, Mehrdad Ashofteh (who is not among us anymore), and Haleh Owzar. I also wish to thank my colleagues at the department of Gender and Women's Studies at UC Berkeley: Barrie Thorne, Charis Thompson, Paola Bacchetta, Laura Nelson, Leslie Salzinger, Trinh Minh-ha, Evelyn Glenn, and Mel Chen for their support.

My family was always there for me. My beloved brother Ali Moallem and my mother Mohtaram Shariatpanahi, who both left me eternally during the last stages of writing this manuscript, helped me with anything I needed, from books and films to care and love. I am also indebted to my sisters, Mehraneh and Mahnaz, and my brothers, Abbas and Ahmad, who never failed to support me. My husband and *yar*, Shahin Bayatmakou, was always there for me, personally and intellectually. My son Arash, with his heroic recovery from a life-changing accident during the writing of this book, made me believe even more in the importance of material and immaterial labor. I dedicate this book to him, to his courage, perseverance, strength, and to his commitment to making life a journey to be celebrated every single day even under challenging circumstances.

Last but not least, this book would not have been possible without many conversations with weavers, traders, sellers, and consumers of carpets from the Lut desert to Tehran, Paris, London, Los Angeles, and San Francisco. Without these conversations, I would not have been able to grasp the complexity of the Persian carpet as a commodity. The pages of this book cannot embrace all those exchanges.

INTRODUCTION

Attachments

Figure 0.1 **Commodity**
Karkas/Shutterstock.com

For those of us from the middle class who lived in Iran, carpets are an important part of the material world in which we were raised. Carpets are important objects in the process of our subject formation, if we understand subject formation to be about habitus, taste, aesthetic pleasures, class distinctions, consumerism, affects, and the tactile and sensory memory of material objects.[1] I was raised with carpets as a child, since carpets were part of "things we inherited" and things that people regularly replaced or added to their household.[2]

New home decoration in the 1960s used industrial carpeting in Iran, but my family, like many others, remained loyal to carpets.[3] My father loved to buy carpets—sometimes out of passion for them, their colors, and their designs, and sometimes because someone asked him to buy them to help a weaver. As a modernized woman, my mother was less concerned about the carpets and more about how the household looked. She was suspicious of anything old-looking (at some point she even replaced all our old carpets with new ones), since to her anything old was a manifestation of something called "traditional." However, carpets were the first commodities that connected me to my class positionality and made me aware of the linkage between consumption and production.

As an undergraduate student at Tehran University working on a research project in Isfahan villages, I became aware of the conditions in which carpet weavers in familial workshops were living. I came to be fascinated with the songs they were improvising when weaving the carpets, and I started to collect them. They told stories about hard work, sometimes ridiculing and mocking those who exploited the weavers, many of whom were women and young girls, and occasionally young boys.

The carpet is a material object and a commodity that defines and influences the habitus of those who either live in the cultural sphere where carpets are part and parcel of everyday life or come into contact with the carpet as a material object. Learning how these beautiful Isfahan carpets were produced connected me to the fact that some of us owned carpets at the expense of others who were working under very harsh conditions. It made it impossible for me to think about aesthetics and consumerism without thinking about the labor as well as the materiality of things consumed. It was hard to enjoy the carpets without remembering the touch of the threads, the sound of the loom, the movement of the skilled, bruised hands and laboring bodies, and the melodies of the songs that made it tolerable for the weavers to live under such exploitative conditions for long hours each day. I became more sensitive to the sound of labor and the melody of long days spent enduring painful work conditions.[4]

After I had become diasporic, it didn't take long for my household to start accumulating carpets again. Each time my relatives visited from Iran, they brought a carpet for me as a gift. Persian carpets were mostly exported to the United States before the Iranian Revolution of 1979. However, the limits of the US embargo on the carpets and the pleasure of having a commodity that transgressed borders and traveled regardless of rules and regulations created a new excitement for possessing the carpets. It even made entrepreneurs and smugglers out of ordinary diasporic families who managed to bring along too many rugs to display in their households. As one of the carpet dealers I interviewed stated, "Many Persian carpets had to change their identification to pass for Afghani carpets to get into the US market."[5] In this context, the desire to purchase and own Persian carpets increased among diasporic Iranians, including me. It also pushed many carpet entrepreneurs to relocate their workshops to other parts of the world, including India, Pakistan, and China, where they could access a cheap labor force without experiencing the restrictions on importing and exporting that were imposed on carpets from Iran. Youssef Ibrahim describes the dislocation of the labor from Iran to other parts of the world in terms of the magic that has left the Persian carpet.[6] In his view, the relocation of the carpet production outside Iran has ruined its uniqueness. For me, carpets took on a different meaning after I became diasporic. They became a spatialized site of my Iranian identity, because stepping on them daily reminded me of my Iranian-ness and my sensory connection to another place, somewhere far from the United States but in proximity to my embodied sense of belonging.

For many immigrant communities, memory of home and homeland or expressions of belonging are conveyed through tactility and the sensation of one's consumptive practices, from furniture to food to clothing. As noted by Gaston Bachelard, "Our house is our corner of the world. As has often been said, it is our first universe, a real cosmos in every sense of the word."[7] The public and the private converge with each other through consumption of the carpets. Lauren Berlant notes that the public sphere is an affective world, so one cannot avoid attachment to objects and to commodities. In my view, attachment to commodities is part of what Berlant identifies as affective relations based on the continued fantasies of the good life (as it becomes more and more out of reach) in the context of a precarious neoliberal order.[8] The relationship between citizens and the public sphere is increasingly mediated by commodities. Linking political economy with consumerism, Bernard Stiegler describes this process as

> the new form of proletarianization consisting in the organization of consumption as the destruction of savoir-vivre with the aim of creating available purchasing power, thereby refining and reinforcing that system which rested on the destruction of savoir-faire with the aim of creating available labor force.[9]

In other words, proletarianization in consumer capitalism gradually dispossesses the social subjects from their knowledge of doing, living, imagining, and theorizing.[10]

Commodities are crucial in our lives. They are part of our conscious or unconscious memory. They impact our perceptions of a good life, our sense of security, and our sense of connectedness in space. They influence our ideas of beauty, comfort, and identity. They also construct us as particular subjects who bring these commodities into our lives and relate with them affectively.

These everyday relationships to material culture in general and commodities in particular are more unconsciously than consciously constructed. There is no explicit disciplinary rule based on language and socialization that governs these relations; rather, tactile and sensory forms of disciplining occur through material and visual cultures. People come to comprehend their world through commodities that are not produced and represented by a single culture or locality, given that colonial modernity and the transnational globalization of trade and consumerism occurred through cultural encounters.[11] As Karl Polanyi has stated, the two-sidedness of trade involves the meeting of different communities with the purpose of exchanging of goods.[12]

As we are bound to the world of commodities more than ever under consumer capitalism, objects present us with a world of meanings to be interrogated, not only regarding one's attachments but also how our desire for the world we live in could be changed, transformed, and redirected. In this book, I focus on the emergence of the Persian carpet as a modern commodity, from its mid-nineteenth-century upsurge as a civilizational and imperial commodity to its transformation into a national and diasporic commodity in the present.[13] Using a genealogical approach,[14] I trace how this process was accomplished through a series of discourses that come to us from connoisseur books, magazines, movies, films, images, and websites, or what I call "commodity culture."[15] I argue that Oriental carpets were aestheticized and not only functioned as fetish objects that concealed the labor and conditions under which they were produced but also became what I call mnemonic objects that help people remember what was lost or transformed in colonial modernity and modern capitalism.[16] The carpet has also been used as an aide-mémoire to expose suppressed family relations. For example, Hanan Al-Shaykh, a well-known Lebanese author, in her short story "The Persian Carpet" uses the carpet as a mnemonic object to write about girlhood and the institution of marriage and family relations.[17]

One way of linking the history of a commodity with the history of labor is to bring the spectacle of the commodity into conversation with the spectacle of labor. In other words, questions of labor and capital cannot be separated from the aesthetic and affective collective experiences of the everyday and popular culture. As a result, culture and economy are closely linked through consumerism and commodity circulation. In this context, questions of political participation, social resistance, and social transformations require a deep understanding of the intersection of labor, capital, and systems of representation. By focusing on carpets as transnational commodities, I hope to explore further the ways commodities animate social relations of production and consumption, and challenge the idea that the modern subject has risen above the inanimate world of commodities.

Civilizational Commodities

Persian carpets emerged as mass-produced commodities at the end of the nine-teenth and in the early twentieth centuries. This is not to claim that the carpets did not exist as luxury items before their emergence as modern commodities. I use the concept of commodity to refer to three ideas: commodity as an object of material culture, commodity as an object invested with value, and commod-ity as an object of circulation and exchange in the marketplace. Here I distin-guish my approach from those who have written about the carpet as a historical object, tracing the history of the carpet rather than the genealogy of it as a commodity.

The commodification of Persian carpets coincided with the expansion of the marketplace under colonialism and capitalism; the concomitant transnationali-zation of labor, capital, and commodities; and the systems of representation that moved within and beyond national borders and orders. The commodification of the Persian carpet, I argue, has to do with its "commodity context," meaning the particular historical context within which the carpet became a commodity and the current context within which the Persian carpet remains a commod-ity, given that commodities come in and out of the market. As Appadurai has clarified, commodities are not the same as products; they are "things with a par-ticular type of social potential."[18] Furthermore, as Simmel has argued, value is never an inherent property of objects but rather a judgment made about them by subjects.[19]

It is impossible to talk about carpets as commodities without referring to the classic work of Karl Marx in *Capital* and his definition of commodity. Marx makes a direct connection between labor and commodities by defining the latter as "congealed quantities of human labor." In his view, a commodity is "any useful thing that has been rendered available for exchange with other commodities by application of human labor."[20] What is crucial to consider in Marx's definition is the fact that a commodity is a product of human labor and, as a result, is a sensuous thing. However, once it emerges as a commodity, it transcends sensuousness and exists among other commodities. Marx calls this process "commodity fetishism," referring to the ways in which the commodity conceals any trace of the factory, mass production, and the exploitation of the workers. Commodity fetishism, in his view, triumphs as a spectacle of images and beliefs.

I find Marx's definition of commodity fetishism enlightening, especially when it comes to the concealment of labor in the fetish, and the fetish as a site of both external and internal boundary marking. Nevertheless, I argue that Marx's the-oretical framework is influenced by a modernist separation of the image from matter, the subject from the object, and the mediatic from the materialist. To distance myself from that model, I am not referring to fetishism in its pejorative and fear-of-provoking sense, as it has been used since colonial modernity and in European traders' depictions of West African societies as irrational and superstitious, but fetishism as a site of scholarly curiosity not interrupted by the anthropomorphism of modernity.[21]

Taking a deconstructionist approach, I criticize the language of political economy as relying on a system of oppositions between ideas and matter, infrastructure and superstructure, and culture and economy. As we see with the Persian carpet, traveling images and texts make the commodity into a spectacle, in addition to turning the labor that produces that commodity into a spectacle—one that has the potential to both *conceal* and *reveal* at the same time. I make the case for a chain of connectivities that have the possibility to be interrupted at any point.[22]

Kajri Jain notes that fetishism "came through the 19th century via the discourses of anthropology, art, psychoanalysis, and political economy, [and] came to describe the 'primitive' other but to index the (disavowed) otherness *within* the bourgeois subject and liberal political economy."[23] For example, for Freud, the possibility of a corporeal, affective, desiring engagement with an inanimate object was part of perverse sexuality; and for Marx, anxiety about the ways in which objects may come to embody and replace relationships between people contributed to his notion of a commodity as congealed labor. For Marx, the animation of commodities displaces the locus of value production in social labor-time. In other words, the labor-time that is producing value becomes imperceptible. This separation, which Marx depicted as commodity fetishism, refers to an anthropomorphic moment within the context of colonial modernity when the human subject emerges as the individual possessing the object, not being possessed by it. In this context, it is not desire but sensuous desire that generates value. Thus, exceeding the distinctiveness of the immediate sensuous world, a commodity becomes a fetish that congeals labor, as defined by Marx, but it also, as I will argue, stands for the primitive Other.[24] My goal, then, is to bring questions of representational practices into conversation with questions of labor via Persian carpets. I argue that it is crucial to interrogate the relationship between materiality and immateriality and the ways in which both constitute labor processes and consumer culture.

Given this line of inquiry, I am less interested in the structuralist obsession with history and more interested in an interrogation of the ways in which value is produced and invested in certain commodities through what some scholars call an assemblage of heterogeneous forces at a particular historical moment.[25] My focus in this book is more on the ways in which, as systems of signs and meanings, in Baudrillard's terms,[26] both imperial and national discourses invest value in carpets as images, aestheticized objects, and representations. Once the carpet became a commodity with exchange value, it also became a transportable, nonhuman agent that interacts with both the text and the context in which it circulates.

In the case of semi-colonized societies like Iran, analytically speaking, the concept of informal imperialism or informal empire enables us to study the complex relations, both formal and informal, between Euro-American powers in cosmopolitan areas and post/semi-colonized or colonized societies in various parts of the world. I suggest that colonial modernity created the possibilities for vision to be disciplined, for technology to channel vision to manipulate it, and for the economy to make vision into a value-producing machine. The Persian carpet as a transnational commodity links the politics of vision with the politics of labor. In other words, it brings political economy, cultural politics, and aesthetics into the same frame of reference. To understand the intersection of modern disciplinary practices with the apparatus of social control and the process of subject formation, we need to transcend the separation of subjects and objects when we think about modernity.

Since 2008, with the expansion of digital networks, we are increasingly witnessing an economy of hyper material, in Stiegler's terms.[27] While earlier Marxist and materialist feminist approaches were concerned with questions of political economy, including the sexual division of labor, they dismissed questions of cultural meanings and immaterial labor. Feminist cultural studies approaches, on the other hand, have relied more on representational practices, while abandoning the question of labor. In this book, I use the Persian carpet as an object of study to bring questions of fantasy, desire, and consumption into conversation with the questions of labor, technology, and the politics of representations to interrogate the affects, attachments, detachments, and disposability of both commodities and labor.

Even though these transnational commodities have penetrated the spaces of everyday life in the West, they still function as fetishes or border objects, crossing the boundaries between bodies and things and perpetuating the notions of self and Other. The consumption of things Oriental not only made the Orient tangible and tactile but also collectible. In this book, I depart with the concept of Orientalia to refer to a series of goods that I call "civilizational commodities." Orientalia in the colonial discourse included any material object attributed to what was referred to as Oriental, Muhammadan, Musulman, and Persian. The concept denotes the boundaries of civilized and primitive, modern and traditional, and industrial and domesticated. In this context, print culture, including connoisseur literature, and visual media such as films, photography, and advertisements were crucial in promoting consumerism around Orientalia. But the impact goes much farther than consumerism. Through the example of the Persian carpet, I also illustrate how the symbolic value invested in a specific commodity in colonial modernity became a site of knowledge accumulation that provided space for the formation of national identity and diasporic ethnicity.

Art, Craft, or Commodity?

Persian carpets are everywhere. They are art objects, crafts, and commodities.[28] They come in different shapes and colors and are both handmade and machine made. They are in homes, hotels, universities, castles, mosques, and museums. They are laid on the ground and hung on the walls, horizontally and vertically, and are used as ornaments, furniture items, sacred objects, and war memorials. It would be difficult to depict a complete picture of the Persian carpet in this book, so, like many other scholars, I am interested in going beyond the dichotomous representation of objects and subjects to focus more on their relationality.

Although carpets have been an object of trade between Iran and the West since the sixteenth century, the Persian carpet became a mass-produced commodity and major export to the West in the late nineteenth century.[29] The carpet is indeed a commodity that moves around quite often. It is as important as a boat or a ship in our modern imagination.[30] Foucault uses the idea of heterotopia to emphasize the importance of the ship as connected to imaginary possibilities as well as movement through space. Though heterotopias are necessary to the order of things, in his view they are also dangerous because they display the continual impossibility of closure. Carpet is a heterotopia. As Dumm notes, "The heterotopia transgresses boundaries as a moment of freedom."[31] For Foucault, "Transgression incessantly crosses and recrosses a line which closes up behind it in a wave of extremely short duration, and thus it is made to return once more right to the horizon of the uncrossable."[32]

The Persian carpet connects different worlds: production and consumption, labor and leisure, and matter and the immaterial, along with the East and the West, without finality. As a commodity it moves in space, but its localization continuously integrates a form of extension, a relation to other sites. In other words, to understand the carpet as a commodity, one needs to go beyond its localization as it spreads and extends to the other locations. What I mean by extension here is the ways in which the carpet spills over its frame aesthetically, requiring a new configuration of time and space. It is an everyday commodity but also a phantasmatic object. As Foucault argues, the carpet represents an "enacted utopia," a heterotopia or a placeless space, that enables us to think about reality.[33] Furthermore, it is an in-between object, not entirely defined by art, crafts, or the world of commodities.

As art, the identity of the Persian carpet has been more ambiguous given its categorization as a furniture item. The oldest ones are museumized as part of the "Islamic art and civilization" sections of European and US museums. Most of the time, they are displayed as things of the past, as things from a civilization that does not exist anymore,[34] or perhaps a civilization stuck in the "anachronistic space" of the past, in Anne McClintock's terms.[35] Even as furniture items, carpets have been poorly categorized. As the author of a *Hali* magazine editorial points out, "Until the mid-1970s, many rugs, however fine or beautiful or important, found themselves poorly described and added either at the beginning or end of a furniture catalogue."[36]

Persian carpets are distinguished from other carpets because of their high quality, defined by the number of knots, or high-knot density, made and tied by hand, which ranges from 40,000 to even 600,000 knots per square meter. As a commodity, the carpet is characterized by its "Oriental" and Persian cultural difference, given that its advertisement is linked to the values generated by the discourses of Orientalism and exoticism. It is a gendered commodity given that gender hierarchies are produced and sustained through both their consumption and production processes. While Persian carpets are largely created through the work of women and children, men control their circulation, trade, and marketing. Their ownership is also characterized as masculine, though they are advertised as feminized commodities juxtaposed with the image of a woman or with the figure of female carpet weavers at the loom. Their distribution is massively reliant on transnational connections and networks of production, trade, advertisement, and consumption beyond the territorial boundaries of nation-states. Their marketing uses "mediatic" spaces and cyberspace to target consumers in new and unprecedented ways that are favorable to trading day and night. They have a unique status as both a work of art, with an aura available for museumization, and a commodity open to marketization, replication, cheap copies, and even post-Fordist forms of production. They also function as "paradoxical spaces" connecting the domestic with the market, production with consumption, the inside with the outside, and the material with the imaginary, conveying the idea of being at home in a highly mobile world.

Indeed, the story of the Persian carpet as an art object, a thing, and a commodity since colonial modernity crosses the boundaries of various countries, cultures, historical periods, and academic disciplines. It registers multiple encounters culturally and aesthetically and multiple border crossings. Given the nature of the international division of labor, generalizing the Persian carpet as "Oriental" is reductive. Persian carpets have a unique history and genealogy that makes their production, circulation, or consumption hard to limit to Iran. On the surface, Persian carpet design includes a hybrid assemblage of symbols and signs from various cultures.

Though the focus of this book is on the Persian carpet as a commodity, it would be difficult to separate out the categories of art, crafts, and commodities because the Persian carpet is all of these at the same time. The most antique carpets have been collected, exhibited, and museumized. Both the handwoven craft carpets and their mass-produced and machine-made counterparts are produced alongside each other. In the modernist traditions that became popular in Iran before the Iranian Revolution of 1979, the separation of art from crafts and commodities marginalized Persian carpets as art.[37] This dichotomy only began to be challenged in the mid-1970s, when the artists associated with the "Saqqa khaneh" school of painting started to pay attention to the carpets as both a vernacular motif in their painting as well as an object of artistic innovation. The establishment of the carpet museum in Tehran in 1976 was the first step in the vernacularization of the carpets as artistic objects. This movement continued with the establishment of a Culture and Art Foundation, including a small museum in Tehran in 1996 for the carpet designer, weaver, and painter Rassam Arabzadeh and the aesthetic depiction of Persian carpets in Iranian films as an indigenizing motif. In one of his interviews with an art journal, Arabzadeh makes a case for the replacement of what is referred to as the carpet industry by the art of carpet weaving that remains anonymous, disconnecting the industry from the art by romanticizing and spiritualizing weaving as "Knots of Love."[38] He writes:

I attribute this anonymity to the art of weaving as an act of love. When one is in love, one becomes quiet avoiding showing off and pretension. The carpet weavers in Iran are some of the most deprived and expelled artists. If you were a weaver at the loom, you would have known what I am referring to. The first row, the second, the third, there is the movement of hands similar to Sama[39] a form of contemplation, passion and excitement. These artists disappear in the formal traces of what is called art since they produce an art that is prone to theft and displacement.[40]

As for the design of the carpets, it is perhaps the most complicated dimension in the process, given that most designs are neither registered nor owned by anyone except for those that are owned by a company or an individual in the Global North. Although production has increasingly been moved around and outsourced to countries where labor is the cheapest and most flexible, especially in the Global South, the patenting of designs is mostly located in the Global North. Because many designers considered their designs as part of the "commons," not possessed by any individual or collectivity, they were copied and transported to the West at the end of the nineteenth century when symbolic commodities started to have a value. I came across an archive of many designs in England created by European travelers who came back with sketches and outlines mimicking carpets, murals, and mosaics.

It would be impossible to tell the story of the designs, then, without telling the story of the transnational theft of those anonymous designs.[41] The commodity nature of the carpets made them more vulnerable to such cultural and international theft.

From Imperial Commodification to Persian-ness

The structure of imperial Europe included material culture that required the circulation of commodities.[42] Mark Crinson's conception of "informal imperialism" is key to this story. Crinson defines informal empire as a "form of imperialism by which control was established through ostensibly peaceful means of free trade and economic integration."[43] The theoretical concept of informal imperialism makes transnational linkages between culture and economy; they are not distinct processes but are interconnected through discourses, institutions, and social subjects. In this context, a nation-state may control a territory without exercising sovereignty.[44] This form of imperialism still persists and involves modes of knowledge production in the age of global media and new information technologies.[45] Thus, it is also crucial and relevant to the present to interrogate the complicity of the nation and the empire in entertainment and consumerism.

In this book, I examine why Persian carpets became a commodity in the context of empire and, later on, in the process of nation formation in Iran. It is also crucial to ask why people keep buying Persian carpets to this day, and how they appeal to masses of consumers. Ultimately, I argue that the key to answering these questions is in understanding how the Persian carpet's transformation from an imperial commodity into a sign of Persian-ness, with its investment in the eternity of history and identity, exists both temporally and spatially in the historical time of colonial modernity and postmodernity.

To illustrate this transformation, I focus on representational practices in a number of sites, including Orientalist films, connoisseur books, advertisement, and websites in the nation and diaspora. I show how a visual economy around commodities from the so-called Orient works to invest value in the Persian carpet. These types of representation have been crucial in creating a form of what I call "affective consumption." I define affective consumption as a more communitarian act based on consuming less by conscious knowing but influenced by forces of encounters between various actants (subjects, objects, discourses, institutions, etc.).[46] We are never alone when we consume something affectively, or as Sara Ahmed puts it, the social bond is always sensational and "affect is what sticks."[47] Connectivity is the key word here. This affective connection to others has been colonized and appropriated by the imperialist consumption of the Other, while it has also created space for the re-appropriation and nationalization of Persian carpets as a form of cultural heritage, a claim to Persian-ness as a site of we-ness.

In the context of diaspora, the visible presence of ethnic things is either limited to specific neighborhoods, particular stores, or communal and religious areas. These objects and spaces are at times exoticized and controlled, and on other occasions contested and contained. Controversies over the building of a mosque or a cultural center for Muslim communities in New York, the construction of minarets in Europe, or the construction of Asian-designed houses in Vancouver are expressions of xenophobia and Islamophobia. While diasporic food seems to have had an easier time integrating into the mainstream cultures of the majoritarian groups, clothing and home design have been used more as an affirmation of identity.[48] The memory and sensuality that material objects manifest become expressions of sociality and the politics of affect in encounters between social subjects.

Vision and Value

"We regret, hope, fear, and love with images."

John Berger, "Another Way of Telling,"
Journal of Social Reconstruction 1, no. 1 (1980): 73

Theories of cultural studies are crucial to our understanding of representational practices, which are an integral part of the economy. However, there is a gap in the link between cultural representations and the political economy. To overcome this theoretically, I propose the concept of the "scopic economy"[49] to bring into conversation notions of vision with questions of value in commodity circulation. While vision is central in representation, value is crucial to economic exchange. The fetishism of commodities via the technologies of vision, including photography, film, and digital media, not only produce value but also the memory of touch or tactility.[50] Value is accumulated through the repetition of the image as well as its re-designation in the production of new symbolic and material value as we move from a modern culture of speed to a postmodern culture of immediacy. So, it would be impossible to rely on transnational cultural studies without bringing it into conversation with historical materialism and the political economy.

As a theoretical concept, the scopic economy runs through each chapter to bring culture and economy into conversation with each other. The scopic economy is crucial for tracing those regimes of visibility that enabled the construction of a commercial empire in Europe and then the United States, the formation of nation-states, and the creation of transnational, imperial, and national economic networks.[51] The concept brings to the fore the important traffic between Europe, the United States, and the so-called Orient through the juxtaposition of taste, desire, consumerism, commodity fetishism, and labor.[52] I argue that the scopic economy is mediated through regimes of curiosity as well as modes of surveillance that produce both attachment to and detachment from the commodities. Indeed, the scopic economy functions as a modus operandi that constitutes social practices related to the production, exchange, and consumption of commodities. More specifically, the scopic economy is a spectacle that privileges seeing, those affects that produce an attachment to and a detachment from an object in a regime of signification, and a performative subject that bonds with possessions as she/he looks while being watched. Commodities provoke affects and sentiments, or what Lori Merish calls a form of "sentimental materialism,"[53] combined with the act of seeing from an embodied position and setting in motion a series of activities that explains consumptive production. In other words, the scopic economy includes images, tropes, and signifiers along with commodities as part of a regime of curiosity, in Stephen Bann's terms,[54] as they cause commodification and de-commodification.

Objects and commodities are not the same. Indeed, the genealogy of the Persian carpet as a commodity goes back to the late nineteenth century. Leonard Helfgott, the author of one of the most comprehensive studies of Persian carpets, writes, "While carpets have been an object of trade between Iran and the West since the seventeenth century, the Persian carpet did not become a major export to the West until the late nineteenth century."[55] To understand the genealogy of the Persian carpet as a commodity, I elaborate on the rules of textual formation that discursively constitute a commodity, in this case, the Persian carpet. I explain how the Persian carpet became a commodity candidate and which discourses determined the value of this particular object. I also elaborate on the commodity context of the Persian carpet and explain how one's desire for an object is fulfilled by giving up of other objects. In other words, the process of commodification of some objects may involve de-commodification of other objects. For example, the mass production of Persian carpets put an end to the making of cotton and silk in Iran.

Elaborating further on the scopic economy of the Persian carpet, I show how and in which ways this economy functions through the spectacle of labor. I demonstrate how particular ideas of otherness portray a feminine figure, as in the example of Orientalist and nationalist discourses. In my prior book, *Between Warrior Brother and Veiled Sister*, I extensively explored the regimes of visibility in the modern systems of gendered citizenship in Iran. However, in this work, I am more interested in the politico-economic processes that involve an aestheticization of objects and a scopic economy beyond issues of citizenship.

Indeed, we cannot separate the genealogy of investing value in certain commodities, images, icons, and tropes from the sociohistorical context within which these value judgments are made. As economic historians Brewer and Porter demonstrate, new middle-class politics are extensively linked to consumerism and the emergence of what they call *homo edens* or the consumer.[56] However, as Mark Paterson notes, the consumer cannot be reduced to *homo economicus*,[57] or the paradigmatic rational consumer, and market value not only reflects cultural values but also, in my view, can mobilize consumptive production. For example, in the scopic economy, social relations of power based on race, gender, nation, class, and culture systematically employ difference (especially the iconography of a feminine Other).

The employment of difference guarantees modes of subjectification that create a unity between the subject of seeing and the location from which one sees, enabling identification and disidentification within a particular commodity culture. This form of mediation and mediatization functions through what Latour describes as "a whole cycle of accumulation: how to bring things back to a place for someone to see it for the first time so that others might be sent again to bring other things back, how to be familiar with things, people, and events, which are distant."[58] This process creates not only a circuit of bodies, objects, and information but also a constant need for mediation and for bringing things, events, and people into the realm of visibility and representation.[59] In this case, to be in the realm of the visible through identification is inseparable from the discourses of mediation, practices of seeing and displaying, and affective consumption. That is why the politics of representation cannot be limited to the temporality of here and now, disconnected from the historical context within which they take place, a challenge I present to theories of cultural studies as they come to an understanding of commodification and consumer culture.

To elaborate further on vision and value, I employ a few other concepts regarding the significance of objects in social, cultural, and economic life. It is important to note that transnational commodities, and in this case Orientalia, are unique in the ways they display value as an extension, meaning a relationship to other sites. To understand this process, I elaborate on the significance of mediation and mediatization. I examine commodity aesthetics, or the specific appearance of a commodity, and what Haug calls the "subjective sensuality" through which both subjects of consumption and subjects of production identify with the exchange value of a commodity.[60]

Some scholars refer to the concept of "manipulation" when discussing the significance of representational practices.[61] I find this description reductionist and insufficient to understand this process. While consumers do not all have the same needs and desires, commodities target particular groups by infiltrating the collective imagination based on the binarisms of here/there, past/present, primitive/civilized, home/market, manual/intellectual, female/male, and finally spiritual/material. I build upon the concept of "commodity aesthetics" suggested by Haug to highlight the connection between the economic and the aesthetic. In other words, I refer to the Persian carpet both as a commodity that appeals to our senses as an object of beauty that has developed since colonial modernity in the service of exchange value.[62]

The nature of commodity aesthetics and their appeal to a broad range of consumers and producers sustains a subjective sensuality that maintains the order of things. Also, the mediating and mediatizing process within which these commodities are aestheticized, circulated, and consumed valorizes capital as a necessity and commerce as the infinite site for the embodied inhabitation of the space. Deleuze and Guattari note that the field of the political creates an opposition between possibilities of movement and control over a territory. In this context, transnational commodities resolve this contradiction by displaying a world of shared sociality and mutual continuity with the paradoxical presence of mobility as the global leveling of the space of goods with the uneven and unequal places of confined labor.

Methodological Fetishism

I started to work on the topic of Oriental carpets in general and Persian carpets in particular more than a decade ago. I traveled to numerous locations from San Francisco to Los Angeles, Berlin, Paris, Lyon, Kidderminster, London, Istanbul, and many carpet-producing locations in Iran. I learned enormously about the Persian carpets' complex designs, technics, and regional variations, through this research. I interviewed weavers, dealers, collectors, carpet entrepreneurs, and consumers of carpets in many locations. A number of times I visited a village in the Lut Desert of Iran where most women are involved in carpet weaving. I refer to this village using the pseudonym of Talie Abad. I also did archival research at the Musée des Tissus et des Arts Décoratifs de Lyon, L' Institute du Monde Arabe, the Bibliothèque Nationale de la France, the Carpet Archives in Kidderminster (England), the Advertisement Archive in London, the Textile Museum in Washington DC, Rassam Arabzadeh Foundation and Museum, and the Carpet Museum in Tehran. Given the complexity of Persian carpets as an object of study and my feminist commitment to interdisciplinary methodologies, I combine a few methodological approaches.

First of all, I rely on methodological fetishism, as suggested by Appadurai, to focus all my attention on the "thing" itself rather than sociologizing the transactional moments of the carpet. Shifting the focus of my study from a "human-subject"-centered to a commodity- or thing-centered perspective—a direction that privileges objects, matters, things, and goods—helps me to redirect the scholarly gaze to what is ordinary, banal, lifeless, inanimate, and fetishistic. This form of methodological fetishism does not abandon subjects; indeed, what has constituted subjects more than anything else since colonial modernity is the possession of objects, things, or commodities. As Baudrillard states, "What you collect is always yourself."[63] This shift of focus also enables an orientation towards possessions, avidity, and properties, as Gabriel Tarde notes.[64] Methodologically speaking, I try to go beyond the fetishization of the subject in Marxist approaches, the image in cultural studies, and the word in poststructuralism to bring materiality back into the conversation. In other words, I am interested in the material vitality of the carpet. Like many scholars of new materialism, I am interested in the power that things have, "something active and energetic" in Jane Bennett's words.[65]

The issue of consumerism is critical because it affects the ways in which users/agents/subjects function and operate. As Michel de Certeau argues, "Ways of working or doing things should no longer appear as merely the obscure background of social activity," but rather as related to "a body of theoretical questions, methods, categories, and perspectives that penetrate this obscurity, to make it possible to articulate them."[66] My examination of commodities and everyday life is not a return to the notions of individual taste and questions of consumerism as a choice. It is an attempt to show how, since colonial modernity, everyday modes of operation have included both subjects and objects in the process of the production and consumption of commodities. By putting into action operational discourses that convey distinct meanings, I wish to bring culture and economy into the same frame of reference. Crucial in this context are the notions of choice and value involved in these modes of operation, in the most common sites of cultural and material production, including commodity culture, interior design, advertisement in museums, connoisseur books, bazaars, shopping malls, art galleries, cyber zones, ethnic TV ads, and auctions.

My second methodological approach is feminist transnational cultural studies, given that representational practices and the circulation of images are central to this study. However, to grasp transnational connectivities, I introduce the notion of extension to engage the local, the global, and the transnational. I argue that the dichotomy of the local and the global has prevented us from studying the ways each site extends to other places, explaining that locations are indeed both places and spaces. Doreen Massey refers to both place and space in terms of social relations or as constituted by social relations,

> constructed out of a multiplicity of social relations across all spatial scales,
> from the global reach of finance and telecommunications, through the

geography of the tentacles of national political power to the social relations within the town, the settlement, the household and the workplace.[67]

Massey refers to the notion of place as a particular moment of those networks of social relations. The notion of extension, in my view, resonates with Massey's notion of place by showing how the story of commodities is always translocational and transnational but also methodologically traceable in the sense that no matter where one starts an inquiry and in which particular moment in time, one ends up moving in space and time through extension and connectivity.

Third, I supplement methodological fetishism and transnational feminist cultural studies with ethnography and interviews with weavers, traders, consumers, and collectors in various sites. Though I do not call this book an ethnographic work in traditional anthropological terms, I am informed by my conversations with different social agents involved in the carpet industry from consumption to production and vice versa.[68] I interviewed weavers, dealers, traders, and consumers in several locations, including Iran, France, Germany, England, Australia, and the United States (from Los Angeles to the Bay Area), from 2007 to 2016. To offer a deeper understanding of how this transnational network functions, I weave ethnographic materials with other forms of evidence.

Although there is a significant body of literature in recent years that focuses on things and objects, less research has been done on the process of the commodification of particular objects from a transnational perspective.[69] Also, the field is still wide open for an illustration of the genealogy of specific objects and their connection to the formation and transformation of both nation and empire. That is why this book focuses on one single commodity, the Persian carpet, as a transnational commodity, to depict the complexity of this story and the conditions under which an object makes it to the world of commodities. Moving with the carpet as a commodity, I have been taken to different places—museums, libraries, villages, and bazaars—traveling from Kidderminster in England to Lyon in France to Isfahan in Iran—from one location to another, discovering a new link in each place. Without linking the emergence of the Persian carpets as a commodity and the transformation of the carpet industry in Kidderminster at particular historical moments to a multiplicity of power relations beyond those specific places, it would be difficult to accomplish a transnational analysis.

As a feminist scholar, I believe that it is crucial to bring the space of economy into conversation with the spectacle of labor to be able to understand the continuous production and reproduction of feminized exploitative labor in our global and transnational context. I find a tradition of Marxist feminism and materialist feminism in what Guillaumin calls "our ideologically split consciousness" useful to bring gender into conversation with political economy.[70]

However, both of these traditions of feminist theorizing rely on colonial modernity's epistemic frameworks, thus dismissing the relationship between geopolitics and bio-politics, as well as colonization and the mediation of knowledge in regulating power relations. Also, the materialist turn in feminism has remained mostly attached to the position of women in systems of production or reproduction and questions of women as a class. The literature remains vastly invested in the location of power within a male/female or slave/master dichotomy. Apart from some postcolonial feminist scholars including Parama Roy, Caren Kaplan and Inderpal Grewal, Gayatri Spivak, Inderpal Grewal, and Piya Chatterjee, among others for whom questions of labor, capital and systems of representation are central to their theoretical framework,[71] this feminist literature lacks engagement with questions of colonialism, imperialism, and consumerism, where a particular form of liberal individualism intertwines with the liberal culture of humanism and consumerism to produce material positions for the subjects and objects of humanism. Feminist materialism also does not distance itself from the liberal humanist emphasis on the separation of the human from the world of things, overlooking affective flows that connect subjects, objects, beliefs, performances, identities, and actions.

My analytical framework goes beyond the Eurocentric and universalist framework of materialist and Marxist feminism to consider a set of entangled and complex material relationalities by paying close attention to vernacular, national, regional, and global issues. I am mostly interested in what holds things together—for example, what makes feminism compatible with imperialism or what makes consumption consistent with production, or nationalism with imperialism. I believe that the discourse of humanism, the rhetoric of salvation, and the institution of what Laura María Agustín calls the "rescue industry" not only enable an imperialist form of feminism but also create a subject position where the viewer can affectively act upon the viewed.[72]

My research tries to bring politics and culture into conversation with economics from a postcolonial and transnational feminist perspective. In using a transnational feminist approach, not only do I engage humanism in feminism as complicit with the liberal empire, but I also track encounters, exchanges, and the historical conditions that became productive of certain forms of commodities as well as subjectivities. Although I continue to be invested and interested in feminist materialism, I am moving away from the anthropomorphic-centered approach of it. Inspired by the insights of new materialism theories, I look to the sophisticated practices that account for both human and nonhuman entities. Borrowing the concept of "the colonial matrix of power" in decolonial theory,[73] I supplement it with what I call "the imperial matrix of power," or imperiality in Revathi Krishnaswamy's terms, to link colonialism with new forms of imperialism that are dependent on the free market to bring the political economy into conversation with issues of culture and representation in a transnational context.[74] I believe that sites of confinement of feminized labor in our transnational world have not necessarily been located in the factories but continue to function within a complex network of mediations.[75] To understand this emplacement of feminized labor, we must examine how commodity culture and consumerism are monitoring and regulating labor through what Deleuze refers to as short-term and rapidly changing control societies.[76]

Persian Carpet as a Transnational Commodity

My passion for studying Persian carpets started a long time ago, before I became diasporic. The more I reviewed the literature, which mostly focused on carpet weavers and especially on women and children, the more I became critical of colonial and imperialist ideological investments in this kind of writing. Even works by feminist scholars, in keeping with the visual depictions of women and children, depicted carpet weavers as the ultimate victims of a patriarchal order. They left no space for the agency of the weavers, the vitality of the carpets, or the aesthetic pleasures of their consumption. It betrayed the songs my carpet weavers improvised. In these forms of representation, there is no space for the subaltern to be heard. The moralist and humanist framework of this literature and imagery since the nineteenth century, I conclude, is utterly Eurocentric and masculinist, as I will explain in various chapters of this book.

I tell the story of the carpet through five chapters. In the first chapter, I analyze connoisseur books as bodies of knowledge that were crucial for the construction of Oriental carpets in general and Persian carpets in particular. Rarely studied in academia, this informal body of work led to the creation of a decontextualized knowledge where commodities, in this case, the Persian carpet, were represented as disconnected from the circuits of labor and complex hybrid trajectories of cultural meanings. This chapter illustrates how connoisseur books mediate and mediatize the carpet as a commodity.

The second chapter tells the story of the Persian carpets as Orientalia. In this chapter, I map out the commodification of Oriental carpets in the context of the nineteenth and twentieth centuries through the discourse of Orientalism. I specifically follow a few moments at which Orientalist narratives and imaginaries invest value in carpets and put them into circulation. Through an analysis of some examples, including films and advertisement, I show how representational practices glue together an economy of affects with political economy. Orientalia in general and Persian carpets in particular, I argue, are a series of commodities that link consumptive production with productive consumption. The cumulative effect of the first two chapters expounds the genealogy of the carpets as modern commodities. It also shows how the emergence of Persian carpets as commodities intersects with colonial as well as local histories and cultures, and how vision intervenes in creating a spectacle and a field of economic action for productive and consumptive practices.

Chapter 3 develops the story of the carpets by bringing the spectacle of commodities into conversation with the spectacle of labor. It elaborates on the ways in which Orientalization of the carpets and their circulation corresponded with the transnationalization of exploitative feminized labor. Linking the spectacle of commodity to that of the labor, this chapter complicates the spectacularization of the Persian carpets and their intersection with the display of certain laboring bodies. What comes through this intersection more clearly is the ways in which these spectacles serve to naturalize the labor while exoticizing and Orientalizing the carpets.

Chapter 4 focuses on the transformations that took place within the context of nation-state building in Iran. It shows how the discursive shift that occurred during this process turned Persian carpets into national commodities that displayed both the unity and diversity of the Iranian nation. This discursive and institutional shift, I argue, took place gradually and slowly, involving local, national, and transnational elite as well as the mass consumers of Persian carpets. This process was not unilateral, from the top down or the empire to semi-colonies, but involved an assemblage of discourses, institutions, and social agents.

Chapter 5 follows the carpet as it moves in the online marketplace and ethnic TV and internet auctions. I argue that new value and meanings have been invested in the carpet since the mass migration of Iranians to the United States and Europe after the Iranian Revolution of 1979. This chapter winds up delving further into the disconnection between technologies of weaving and modern computing by exposing the militarization of the carpet industry and its techniques of production as separated from the networks of knowledge and power. To elaborate further on this argument, I take up how the hegemonic power of the masculinist history of sciences has separated the history of carpets from the history of computers and foreclosed. Hence, the subordination of women's modes of knowing and doing that cross the boundaries of home/ market, tradition/modern, homeland/diaspora, and non-work and work in the web of life is inseparable from the production of carpets as commodities that represent we-ness and otherness as both affectively desired and disavowed.

Notes

1. I find Sara Ahmed's definition of affect useful. She argues, "Affect does not reside in an object or sign, but is an effect of the circulation between objects and signs (the accumulation of affective value). Signs increase in affective value as an effect of the movement between signs: the more signs are circulated, the more affective they become." Sarah Ahmed, *The Cultural Politics of Emotion* (New York: Routledge, 2004), 45.

2. Carpets were produced as use value before they became arts and crafts and luxury goods. The history of the Persian carpet as an object of art and craft is beyond the scope of this book. According to the famous Orientalist Sir George Birdwood, Persian carpets can be traced to the Achaemenian era. Leonard Helfgott argues that during the fifteenth-century Timurid and Turkman rule, carpets emerged as a commodity. Leonard Helfgott, *Ties That Bind, Social History of the Iranian Carpet* (Washington, DC: Smithsonian Institution Press, 1994), 275. To track this history, some scholars go back to the invasion of Iran by Mongols in the thirteenth century and the devastating effects of the Mongols' destruction of libraries and irrigation systems, arguing that during a period of cultural revival after the establishment of a Mogul Empire that extended to India and Afghanistan and the assimilation of Mogul invaders to the Iranian culture, Iranian painting and tile work along with carpet design flourished. However, the history of Persian carpets as luxury objects goes back to the establishment of the Safavid dynasty (1501 through 1722), when the art, craft, and architecture of Iran became a virtue and a site of royal patronage and started to vastly influence the Mediterranean Islamic world. See Rudolph Matthee, *The Politics of Trade in Safavid Iran: Silk for Silver 1600–1730* (Cambridge: Cambridge University Press, 2000); Roger Savory, *Iran Under the Safavids* (Cambridge: Cambridge University Press, 1980).

3. Commercial floor rugs were used in combination with Persian carpets. Many apartments and houses started to have two-layered carpeting.

4. Most weavers in the handwoven carpets are rural women. See Farhad Nomani and Sohrab Behdad, *Class and Labor in Iran: Did the Revolution Matter?* (Syracuse: Syracuse University Press, 2006).

5. Author interview with a Persian carpet entrepreneur in Paris, April 2011.

6. Youssef Ibrahim, "The Magic Has Left the Persian Carpet," *New York Times*, February 12, 1995.

7. Gaston Bachelard, *The Poetics of Space* (Boston: Beacon Press, 1969), 2–3.

8. Lauren Berlant, *Cruel Optimism* (Durham, NC: Duke University Press, 2011).

9. Bernard Stiegler, *For a New Critique of Political Economy*, trans. Daniel Ross (Cambridge, UK: Polity Press, 2010), 27.

10. Stiegler distinguishes between employment and work. He argues that contrary to the work as transforming the world, all forms of employment are currently being subjected to an irremovable and closed system where the use value has become "une valeur jetable ou pubelisse," or a disposable value. (Interview with Amaelle Guiton entitled "Reconstruire l'économie en redonnant de la valeur au savoir," *Libération*, 8 février 2017.)

11. I refer to colonial modernity to argue that modernity as an era, as a form of consciousness of an era, and as the establishment of modern institutions from nation-states to modern forms of government cannot be separated historically from colonialism and imperialism.

12. Karl Polanyi, "The Economy as Instituted Process," in *The Sociology of Economic Life*, ed. Mark Granovetter and Richard Swedberg (Boulder, CO: Westview Press, 1992), 41.

13. The name "Persian carpet" was given to carpets produced in Iran in the nineteenth century, associating them with the Persian empire.

14. I borrow the concept of a genealogical approach from Michel Foucault. Foucault defines genealogy as distinguished from historical analysis, which is concerned with the study of origins, universality, and historical continuities. For Foucault the focus of analysis in a genealogical approach includes the multiplicity of issues that constitute an event—including the intersection of power and knowledge in constituting systems of domination, subjugation, transgression, and resistance. See Michel Foucault, *Discipline and Punish: The Birth of the Prison* (London: Penguin Press, 1977).

15. Parallel to what Elaine Freedgood calls "thing culture." Elaine Freedgood, *The Ideas in Things: Fugitive Meaning in the Victorian Novel* (Chicago: The University of Chicago Press, 2006).

16. I agree with Thomas Kim's point that "aesthetization renders particular types of observation and objects available to discourse" ("Being Modern: The Circulation of Oriental Objects," in *American Quarterly* 58, no. 2 [June 2006]: 392).

17. She writes: "The lines and colours of the Persian carpet were imprinted on my memory. I used to lie on it as I did my lessons; I'd be so close to it that I'd gaze at its pattern and find it looking like slices of red watermelon repeated over and over again. But when I sat down on the couch, I would see that each slice of melon had changed into a comb with thin teeth. The clusters of Rowers surrounding its four sides were purple-coloured." Hanan Al-Shaykh, "The Persian Carpet," in *Arab Short Stories* (Berkeley: University of California Press, 1994), 109.

18. Arjun Appadurai, ed., *The Social Life of Things: Commodities in Cultural Perspective* (Cambridge: Cambridge University Press, 1986), 6.

19. Georg Simmel, *The Philosophy of Money* (New York: Routledge, 1978).

20. Karl Marx, *Capital. Volume One: A Critique of Political Economy* (London: Penguin Group, 1976[1906]).

21. Alfonso Maurizio Iacono traces the history of the concept of fetish and fetishism to 16th century. He argues that the notion of fetishism emerged as a key concept for a theory of primitive religion in 1760 and with the publication of Charles de Brosses Du Cult Des Dieux Fétiche. See Alfonos Maurizio Iacono, *The History and Theory of Fetishism* (London: Palgrave Macmillan, 2016), 11.

22. As explained by Stuart Hall "Fetishism takes us into the realm where fantasy intervenes in representation; to the level where what is seen, in representation, can only be understood in relation to what cannot be seen, what cannot be shown. Fetishism involves the substitution of an object for some dangerous and powerful but forbidden force." Stuart Hall, ed. *Representation. Cultural Representations and Signifying Practices* (London: Sage Publications, 1997) 266.

23. Kajri Jain, *Gods in the Bazaar: The Economics of Indian Calendar Art* (Durham, NC: Duke University Press, 2007), 223.

24. For an enlightening analysis and critique of Marx's notion of fetishism, see William Pietz, "Fetishism and Materialism: The Limits of Theory in Marx," in *Fetishism as*

Cultural Discourse, ed. Emily Apter and William Pietz (Ithaca, NY: Cornell University Press, 1993), 119–151.

25. Theoretically speaking, a number of scholars refer to Deleuze's concept of *agencements* (translated as assemblage in English) to grasp the interaction between the texts and the worlds as they are reconfigured in terms of the orientation of desire and collective action in specific situations. Assemblages are constituted of heterogeneous elements including bodies, objects, signs, and events that are in a relationship with each other. See, among others, Gilles Deleuze, *Critique et Clinique* (Paris: Les Éditions de Minuit, 1993).

26. Baudrillard, *Simulacres et Simulations* (Paris: Galilée, 1981).

27. Stiegler, *For a New Critique of Political Economy*.

28. The concept of art in Farsi has a more extensive meaning, including knowledge, science, perfection, bravery, virtue, and wisdom. The carpet combines all these ideas going beyond the separation of art, craft, and commodity.

29. Helfgott, *Ties That Bind*, 10.

30. Since colonial modernity, ships have been a signifier of travel, motion, intersection, and transition. Paul Gilroy refers to the ships to illustrate the circulation of ideas, people, and activities in the context of slavery across the Atlantic. See Gilroy, *The Black Atlantic: Modernity and Double Consciousness* (Cambridge, MA: Harvard University Press, 1993).

31. Thomas L. Dumm, *Michel Foucault and the Politics of Freedom* (Lanham, MD: Rowman & Littlefield, 2002), 44.

32. Michel Foucault, "A Preface to Transgression," in *Language, Counter-Memory, Practice: Selected Essays and Interviews*, ed. and trans. Donald F. Bouchard (Ithaca, NY: Cornell University Press, 1977), 34.

33. Michel Foucault, "Des Espace Autres," in *Architecture/movement/Continuité* (Octobre 1984) (based on Foucault's lecture in March 1967).

34. The Persian carpet dealer and connoisseur Cecil Edwards explains his choice of Persian instead of Iranian in the following terms: "Let me say, before proceeding further, that throughout this book I propose to use the older words "Persia" and "Persian," rather than "Iran" and Iranian–the more recent usage. I trust my Persian friends will not be displeased that I have chosen the more venerable forms. I have done so because to me, at least, the word "Iranian"–particularly when applied to the products of the weaver's art–does not suggest the antiquity, the elegance or the renown which the word "Persian" awakens in my mind."(A. Cecil Edwards, The Persian Carpet (London: Duckworth, 1983), V.

35. Anne McClintock, *Imperial Leather: Race, Gender and Sexuality in the Colonial Contest* (New York and London: Routledge, 1995), 41.

36. "Oriental Carpet in Islamic Art," *Hali* 2, no. 1 (Spring 1979), 2.

37. In pre-modern Iranian literature and poetry, the notion of art is used broadly to refer to anything from technology to virtuoso and bravery. The carpet also crossed the boundaries of art, craft, and decorative object in the pre-modern Iranian court and was bartered as a gift, challenging modern notions of authorship and originality.

38. Rassam Arabzadeh, "*Gereh-e'eshq (Knots of Love). A Collection of Fine Artistic Rugs by Master Rassam Arabzadeh* (Tehran: Tehran Naqsheh, 1992).

39. Audition in Sufi practice is composed of dancing, singing, music, and prayer.

40. From an interview with Arabzadeh F. Heshami Razavi edition, *Prospect of Persian Carpet. A Memorial Appreciation of Rassam Arabzadeh* (in Farsi; Tehran: Golshan Publications, 1371/1992), 14.

41. As pointed out by Sally Price such anonymity of so-called Primitive Art "owes much to the needs of Western observers to feel that their society represents a uniquely superior achievements in the history of humanity." Sally Price, *Primitive Art in Civilized Spaces* (Chicago: The University of Chicago Press, 1989) 60.

42. It should be noted that Iran was not directly colonized but still controlled through networks of trade and discourses. Elsewhere I have referred to this form of colonial control as "civilizational imperialism." See Minoo Moallem, *Between Warrior Brother and Veiled Sister: Islamic Fundamentalism and the Politics of Patriarchy* (Berkeley: University of California Press, 2005).

43. Cited by Mona Domosh, *American Commodities in An Age of Empire* (New York: Routledge, 2006), 36. Recent references to the notion of a "trade war" provoked by the Trump administration behold the continuation of informal imperialism.

44. Matthew Brown, ed., *Informal Empire in Latin America: Culture, Commerce and Capital* (Malden, MA: Blackwell, 2008), 3.

45. In Latin American studies "informal imperialism" has been refashioned as a theoretical concept to think about informal and formal empire as a continuum rather than analytically distinct. See Andrew Thompson, "Afterword: Informal Empire: Past, Present and Future," in *Informal Empire in Latin America: Culture, Commerce and Capital*, ed. Matthew Brown (Malden, MA: Blackwell, 2008), 231.

46. Bruno Latour defines actants as anything with an agentic capacity that modifies other actors through a series of actions. *The Politics of Nature*, trans. Catherine Porter (Cambridge, MA: Harvard University Press, 2004), 75.

47. Ahmed's notion of affect as sticky refers to "what sustains or preserves the connection between ideas, values, and objects." "Happy Objects," in *The Affect Theory Reader* (Durham, NC: Duke University Press, 2010), 29.

48. For a discussion of the linkage between affective values and effective modes of economic activities see, Minoo Moallem, "The Immigrant Experience. Affective and effective spheres and issues of race and gender," in *Soundings. A Journal of Politics and Culture*. Issue 11, Spring 1999.

49. Minoo Moallem, "Nation on the Move," (Digital Project Designed by Erik Loyer), *Vectors. Journal of Culture and Technology in a Dynamic Vernacular: Difference* 3, no. 1 (Fall 2007).

50. Laura Marks uses the concept of tactile memory or haptic visuality to describe memories involving all senses. See Laura Marks, *The Skin of Film* (Durham, NC: Duke University Press, 2000), 22.

51. For my work on the regimes of visibility and gendered citizenship in Iran, see Moallem, *Between Warrior Brother and Veiled Sister*.

52. A number of social scientist have written about the intersection of taste with the economy and culture, including Bourdieu, who elaborates on the notion of "symbolic goods" in relation to both material culture and aesthetic knowledge. Pierre Bourdieu, *La Distinction, Critique Sociale du Jugement* (Paris: Editions de Minuit, 1979).

53. Lori Merish, *Sentimental Materialism: Gender, Commodity Culture, and Nineteenth-Century American Literature* (Durham, NC: Duke University Press, 2000).

54. Cited by Kevin Hetherington, *Capitalism's Eye: Cultural Spaces of Commodity* (New York: Routledge, 2007), 17.

55. Helfgott, *Ties That Bind*, 10.

56. John Brewer and Roy Porter, eds., *Consumption and the World of Goods* (New York: Routledge, 1993).

57. Mark Paterson, *Consumption and Everyday Life: The New Sociology* (New York: Routledge, 2006), 3.

58. Bruno Latour, *Science in Action* (Cambridge, MA: Harvard University Press, 1987), 220.

59. The literature on what is called "thing theory" significantly contributes to the study of objects within a Eurocentric epistemological framework yet dismisses questions of race, colonialism, and Orientalism.

60. Wolfgang Fritz Haug, *Critique of Commodity Aesthetics: Appearance, Sexuality and Advertising in Capitalist Society*, trans. Robert Bock (Cambridge: Polity Press, 1986), 4.

61. The work of Adorno, Horkheimer, and other Frankfurt School theorists has been crucial for the understanding of the culture industry and the significance of manipulation in mass media. See "The Culture Industry: Enlightenment as Mass Deception," in *Media and Cultural Studies: Keyworks*, eds. Meenakshi Gigi Durham and Douglas M. Kellner (Hoboken, NJ: Wiley-Blackwell, 2001), 41–72.

62. Haug, *Critique of Commodity Aesthetics: Appearance, Sexuality and Advertising in Capitalist Society*.

63. Cited by Emily Apter, "Dan Graham Inc. and the Fetish of Self-Property," in *The Lure of the Object*, ed. Stephen Melville (New Haven, CT: Yale University Press, 2005), 23.

64. For more information please see Bruno Latour, "Tarde and the End of the Social" In Patrick Joyce (edited by) *The Social in Question. New Bearings in History and the Social Sciences* (London: Routledge, 2002) pp. 117–132.

65. Jane Bennett, *Vibrant Matter: A Political Ecology of Things* (Durham, NC: Duke University Press, 2010), 47.

66. Michel De Certeau, *The Practice of Everyday Life*, trans. Steven F. Rendall (Berkeley: University of California Press, 1988), xi.

67. Doreen Massey, *Space, Place, and Gender* (Minneapolis: University of Minnesota Press, 1994), 4.

68. I used pseudonyms for my interviewees except when they asked me to do otherwise.

69. See, among others, Thorstein Veblen, *The Theory of Leisure Class* (1899); Robert Bocock, *Consumption* (New York: Routledge, 1993); Jean Baudrillard, *La Société de consummation* (Paris: Denoil, 1970) and *De La Séduction* (Paris: Galilée, 1979); Appadurai, ed., *The Social Life of Things*.

70. See Colette Guillaumin, *Racism, Sexism, Power and Ideology* (New York: Routledge, 1995); Christine Dephy, "Un feminism materialist est possible," *Nouvelles Questions Féministes* 4 (Autumne 1982); Nicole-Claude Mathieu, "De la conscience dominée des femmes," *Les Cahiers du GRIF* 29, no. 1 (1984); Danielle Juteau, "From Nation-Church to Nation-State: Evolving Sex-Gender Relations in Québec Society," in *Between Woman and Nation*, eds. Caren Kaplan, Norma Alarcon, and Minoo Moallem (Durham, NC: Duke University Press, 1999), 142–161; Natalie J. Sokoloff, *Between Money and Love: Dialectics of Women, Work and the Family* (Santa Barbara, CA: Praeger, 1980).

71. See Parama Roy, *Alimentary Tracts: Appetites, Aversions and the Postcolonial* (Durham, NC: Duke University Press, 2010); Caren Kaplan and Inderpal Grewal, "Transnational Feminist Cultural Studies: Beyond the Marxism/Poststructuralism/Feminism Divides" in *Between Woman and Nation*, eds. Caren Kaplan, Norma Alarcon, and Minoo Moallem (Durham, NC: Duke University Press, 1999), 349–363; Inderpal Grewal, *Transnational America: Feminisms, Diasporas, Neoliberalisms* (Durham, NC: Duke University Press, 2005); Piya Chatterjee, *A Time for Tea: Women, Labor, and Postcolonial Politics on an Indian Plantation* (Durham, NC: Duke University Press, 2001); Gayatri Spivak, "Can the Subaltern Speak?" in *Marxism and the Interpretation of Culture*, eds. Cary Nelson and Larry Grossberg (Chicago: University of Chicago Press, 1988), 271–311.

72. Laura María Agustín, *Sex at the Margins: Migration, Labour Markets and the Rescue Industry* (London: Zed Books, 2007).

73. See Walter Mignolo, *Local Histories/Global Designs: Coloniality, Subaltern Knowledges, and Border Thinking* (Princeton, NJ: Princeton University Press, 2000).

74. Revathi Krishnaswamy, "Postcolonial and Globalization Studies: Connections, Conflicts, Complicities," in *The Postcolonial and The Global*, eds. Revathi Krishnaswamy and John C. Hawley (Minneapolis: University of Minnesota Press, 2008), 13.

75. Because of its home-based organization, it is hard to get an objective view of the population of women carpet weavers in Iran. However, according to Zahra Karimi, in 1996, more than 91 percent of women industrial workers were in the textile and clothing sector, mainly in carpet weaving. See Zahra Karimi, "The Effects of International Trade on Gender Inequality in Iran: The Case of Women Carpet Weavers," in *Veiled Employment*, eds. Roksana Bahramitash and Hadi Salehi Esfandiari (Syracuse, NY: Syracuse University Press, 2011), 179.

76. Gilles Deleuze, "Postscripts on the Societies of Control," *October* 59 (Winter 1992): 3–7.

1

OBJECTS OF KNOWLEDGE, SUBJECTS OF CONSUMPTION

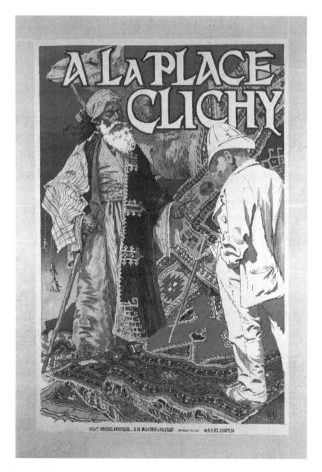

Figure 1.1 **"A La Place Clichy"**
© Victoria and Albert Museum, London

"Hand-woven carpets are, in a sense, the eyesights of thousands of enamored of art thus we step on the eyesight of those in love with it."

> Kazem Shafaghi, "The Carpet Legend Is A Splendid One,"
> in Tehran Times, August 13, 1996, P. 9.

Connoisseur books, as a genre of knowledge production, have been crucial sites for the formation and transformation of material culture and for the production of racial and gendered differences, especially in the modern structure of empire. The genre has led to the creation of a decontextualized knowledge in which commodities like the Persian carpet are disconnected from the circuits of labor and complex hybrid trajectories of cultural meaning. Connoisseur discourses mediated and mediatized Oriental carpets in general and the Persian carpet in particular through the circulation of the carpet as a commodity via photography, advertisements, museum exhibitions, and books. This connoisseur knowledge was supplemented by an intertextual discourse[1] found in journalism and travel writing, both anthropological and feminist, regarding the working conditions and pain that carpet weavers experienced. However, this discourse, which was both constitutive of and constituted by gendered subject positions, mostly served the moral economy of consumerism by uniting pain and pleasure in the commodity in order to influence consumer affect and desires. The transnational circulation of the commodity relied on the discourse of difference in order to produce both subjects of production and consumption. The connoisseur text's interweaving of the tribal female carpet weaver's labor with the sensory and exotic appeal of Orientalia transformed the carpet into a sublime and mobile object.[2]

In this chapter, I map out the commodification of Oriental carpets in the context of the nineteenth and twentieth centuries through connoisseur discourses. These texts circulated an aesthetic education through visual and textual representation, allowing consumers to evaluate and judge the valued from the non-valued. This form of education prepares subjects of consumption with the affect and civilizational optic of empire. This process of mediatization produced the Oriental and Persian carpet as a highly mobile object of desire that attached social subjects to particular notions of time and space, regardless of their location or dislocation within the territorial boundaries of the nation or the empire. The world of carpets and connoisseur literature provides a useful lens with which to examine the significance of knowledge production for the transnational circulation of commodities and the importance of the politics of mediation in the global marketplace.

Persian Carpets and the Gendered Politics of Transnational Knowledge

Originally a luxury item in the Safavid courts of the sixteenth century, the Persian carpet has now joined the assemblage of modern commodities. The importing boom for Oriental carpets began in the late nineteenth century,[3] just around the time when a systematic form of knowledge of these carpets emerged. This knowledge industry, located mainly in France, England, and Germany, brought together academic and nonacademic writing (travelogues, trade guidelines, collectors' books, and exhibition catalogues) in producing the connoisseur book—a particular genre of publication that offered a lush combination of words, pictures, and plates on the exotic appeal of the Persian carpet. This space for cultural and aesthetic knowledge was filled by a vast group of white male specialists, traders, and experts who created the profession of specialized research about the carpet. Oriental and Persian carpets and connoisseur books are a powerful example of how desire and demand for commodity production are created through the politics of value and the politics of knowledge.

Connoisseur books are an important site of the "visualization of knowledge,"[4] which relies on both Eurocentric and masculinist epistemic assumptions.[5] Indeed, as Barbara Stafford argues, this process of opticalization and visualization remains invested in logocentrism and the devaluation of sensory, affective, and kinetic forms of communication.[6] The sheer quantity of connoisseur discourses has, over the years, created an "empire of merchandise."[7] These mediated discourses, originating in print and now carried into newer virtual formats, have enabled the complicity of the nation and empire in the context of a free-market economy and aided the expansion of consumer capitalism beyond the territorial boundaries of nation-states.

Based on my examination of over three hundred books, travelogues, and museum and trade catalogues in English and French (including a number of works translated from German to either French or English and from French or English into Farsi), I elaborate on the convergence of empire and nation in creating pedagogic and affective relations to material objects that are meant to exhibit total mastery of the Other's culture. Focusing on late nineteenth- and early twentieth-century connoisseur texts, I present a genealogy of the carpet in a Foucauldian sense—an evolution of the carpet as a commodity constructed and circulated by these specialized texts.

Connoisseur discourses on the Oriental carpet engage in what Edward Said calls "citationary," nature of Orientalism, referring to a large and varied body of writing that functions by referring repeatedly to itself.[8] Here, I examine not only the constitution of connoisseur expertise but also the technologies within which such expert knowledge could examine, judge, and compare the carpet within the larger frame of knowledge and commodity production. These systems and technologies of organization of the carpet have created a transnational expert knowledge base that links image, information, and experience. This mediation relies extensively on transnational politics of gender and the fetishization of the Other. An examination of the relationship between knowledge and power is crucial for both our understanding of the production of desire for an object as well as the context within which a commodity is produced and exchanged. Questions of exploitation and the feminization of labor are an integral part of the apparatus of politics of knowledge. In the section that follows, I trace the shaping of colonial knowledge production and aesthetic education about the Persian carpet as a decontextualized cosmopolitan commodity.

Commercial Imperialism and Material Culture

While the study of the modern operation of empire through territorial and political claims to power has been central to a critical postcolonial perspective, the story of "informal imperialism,"[9] which includes the complicity of the nation and the empire in entertainment, consumerism, and the military-industrial complex, still needs to be told. This imperialism is mostly established by peaceful means through networks of free trade, consumerism, and economic integration, as well as modes of knowledge production. For example, as Carol Bier argues, the modern production of the Persian carpet cannot be separated from attempts by colonial powers to maintain their dominance in Iran:

> The commercial rivalry between England and Russia grew particularly strong, each evolving a political sphere of influence in Iran. In spite of the complaints of Iranian merchants, European imports reached a peak in Iran in the middle of the nineteenth century. But the decline of textile manufacturing in Iran was difficult to reverse. The most effective effort, however, was that attempted by foreign capitalists who sought to commercialize rug weaving to suit the new demands of the European market. Towards the end of the nineteenth century, investment and capitalization of local and foreign firms in Iran instigated development of the Persian carpet industry. Income from the sale of carpets supplanted that once derived from the export of silk.[10]

The history of commodities is linked to particular temporal and spatial formations and specific modes of economic exchange. Literacy and numeracy[11] have been crucial both in investing value in certain objects as commodities and in making them visible in a regime of calculation, as they are circulated through old and new media and communication technologies. The study of material culture calls for what Van Beek terms "a recognition of materiality in social process, by systematically treating materiality as a quality of relationships rather than things."[12] Connoisseur books are noteworthy for the ways in which they construct the materiality of human interaction and the object in terms of the aesthetic and in terms of "the material process of mediation of knowledge through the senses."[13] In the connoisseur books, the visualization of knowledge is crucial to the life of the commodity. This process of visual literacy includes the optical instruction of the reader's sight or vision, which is formed, educated, and trained to see in particular ways through the mediation of the expert. This process has been influenced by the discourse of commodity as a historical object, of civilizational and cultural difference, and of Orientalism. According to Edward Said, Orientalism is "a mode of discourse with support- ing institutions, vocabulary, scholarship, doctrines, even colonial bureaucracies and colonial styles," dominating, ruling over, and authorizing views of the Ori- ent.[14] The Orient for Said is "the place of Europe's greatest, richest and oldest colonies."[15]

As I have argued in the Introduction, the scopic economy is mediated through the creation of regimes of curiosity as well as modes of surveillance, producing both attachment to and detachment from the object being looked at. Indeed, the scopic economy functions as a modus operandi that constitutes social practices related to the production, exchange, and consumption of com- modities. Here, I show how connoisseurs' texts, academic writing, and adver- tisements, among other items, mediate the politics of value. The concept of scopic economy is crucial for tracing those regimes of visibility that enabled the construction of a commercial empire and the creation of transnational, imperial, and national networks; it brings to the fore the historic traffic between Europe, the United States, and the so-called Orient through the juxtaposition of taste, desire, consumerism, and commodity fetishism.

Connoisseurs, Curiosity, and Culture

I now turn to the regimes of curiosity that produce knowledge by participating in the consumption, circulation, and production of certain narratives, images, signs, tropes, and signifiers. These regimes do not define knowledge either by itself or in opposition to ignorance but, in Latour's words, participate in "a whole cycle of accumulation: how to bring things back to a place for someone to see it for the first time so that others might be sent again to bring other things back. How to be familiar with things, people and events, which are *distant*."[16] Through the mediation of experts engaging in a stylized form of discourse and through the networks of actors connected to these forms of consumption and production, connoisseur discourses forge links between the desire to see and know and practices of belonging.[17] It is these regimes of curiosity that make an object desired, preferred, chosen, and performed, which in turn can influ- ence how an object is linked to the flow of value, either through commodifica- tion or de-commodification. Connoisseurs aided in the development of business practices and changed everyday practices of consumerism through engaging in affective modes of knowledge by deploying active participation in trade, and popularizing anything from collecting objects and traveling to becoming a full-fledged connoisseur. This economy of affects was cumulative and constituted objects and subjects at the same time. It included social subjects that bonded the empire and the nation with affects and passion and created a sense of culture and civilization that was considered to be intrinsic to them.

For example, in a catalogue for the Herr R. G. Hubel Exhibition "Oriental Carpets," we come across statements such as the following:

> The wish to collect artistic objects may be regarded as one of the most attractive human passions. The collector of Oriental carpets combines in his person the hunter, the digger for hidden treasure, the adventurer, and the dedicated researcher. The hunt is exciting until the booty is safely got home. The consequent cherishing, restoring, and preserving of the treasure is a creative activity, which exceeds the mere sentimental contemplation of beautiful objects.[18]

The connoisseur's knowledge is a particular form of knowledge in both its pedagogical directions and its bonding with the object of the trade. C. J. Delabère May regards this knowledge as crucial for every consumer of Persian carpets, claiming,

> With regard to this subject we cannot too strongly urge upon our readers that they must learn to know the rugs themselves before they can really learn to know their values; nor can we over-emphasize the fact that in achieving the ability to correctly identify and classify specimens they will have acquired the chief essential of successful and accurate rug valuation.[19]

The connoisseurs' mediation between consumptive production and productive consumption also generates symbolic capital, which lends both credibility and visibility to the imperial project. Connoisseur knowledge links image, experience, and information through the simultaneous release and confinement of the Other in the pathways of transnational circulation. The relationship between the collector and the trade transcends mere interest in the objects; rather, collectors are portrayed as partaking passionately in the space of connoisseurship. Thus, the connoisseur's affective relationship to the object elevates the carpet as commodity and completes both the cultural and economic circles of meaning. John Gregorian instructs the consumers of the Oriental rugs:

> The most enjoyable and gratifying rugs to own are endlessly enigmatic: there is great pleasure in discovering a hidden motif or a pleasuring color

pattern—even after you've owned the rug for some time. Look for a rug that speaks to your soul. The first rule of thumb when it comes to decorating with Oriental rugs.[20]

The Carpet as a Mobile Commodity and a Historical Object

The carpet as both a sign and a commodity is produced through a historical narrative with a coherent sense of the past, the present, and the future. As represented in this quote,

> Shopping for a Persian rug can be like taking a journey through history. Not only is your rug purchase a fine investment, but in some cultures it is a form of currency! Certainly, it will be a keepsake to hand down from generation to generation. The element of luxury with which Persian rugs are associated today provides a marked contrast with its humble beginning among the nomadic tribes that wandered the great expanses of Persia.[21]

Connoisseur books include illustrations of various carpet designs and carpet-weaving tools along with random pictures of carpet workshops, weavers, and unnamed villages where carpets are produced. The illustrations typically serve as visual supplements to the text without captions. The carpet's status in the present becomes legible through its identification as an object with a historical and almost mythical aura.

As David Sylvester notes in a gallery catalogue on Islamic carpets, "Scholarly collecting—governed by a sense of history—entered the field in the 1870s. Till then, however cherished carpets may have been, little was known about their origins."[22] Indeed, irrespective of the historical fact, connoisseur books depend on narratives of conjecture. Once the carpet is constructed as a sign, a historical object, and commodity, it also becomes a site of differentiation of cultures and civilizations.

In this body of knowledge, the carpet and the people who produce it are both conjoined and separated in terms of their cultural capital. The carpet is considered a primitive craft, but one that has the potential for inclusion in civilized life due to its long history, its Orientalist aura, and its association with religious faith.[23] Cecil Edwards, one the most well-known connoisseurs of the Oriental carpet, remarks:

> The Persian people are by nature skilled and artistic craftsmen. Such a people would not for long remain content to cover their tent floors—like

Eskimos or Red Indians—with the skin of beasts. The urge to fashion something closer to the need, more varied and above all more colorful, was there.[24]

However, even the choice of colors is essentialized and Orientalized. For example, Nicolas Fokker writes, "The favorite colors of the Oriental are orange, the color of religious submission, and turquoise."[25] The historical narrative rehearses modern anthropological notions of civilized and primitive material production as sequences in the history of progress. In one of the earliest connoisseur books, *Rugs of the Orient* (1911), C. R. Clifford writes:

Simple design has been inspired always by primitive thought in so many remote countries that it discourages any logical analysis. In some cases, it seems as though these varying geometrical shapes sprung from the extraordinary mosaics in Byzantine, but a child can take a square or octagon and by drawing from various points intersecting lines evolve innumerable designs. It is primitive world thought.[26]

A linear progression from simple to complex, child to adult, primitive to civilized in terms of artistic and material production serves as a basic assumption in the formation of technical knowledge on the Oriental carpet. In the connoisseur's modes of knowledge production, the focus is on three modes of understanding the carpet: as an object of domestic Orientalia and home design, distinct from the carpet as an antique object; as a commodity displaying cultural difference located within an evolutionary path from primitiveness to civilization; as a product of specific carpet-weaving technologies that are described in great detail and depicted as an extension of nature, radically distinct from modern technological evolutions. Each connoisseur book repeats either the technical details or a descriptive account of the carpet: the wrap, the floral motif, the decoration of the border. The fascination with the techniques of carpet weaving—the loom, the raw materials, the colorants, the knots, the wefts, and the warp—conceals the collaborative work involved in carpet weaving, including the cooperation between various forms of labor and networks of help, sociability, and solidarity. In this context, carpet weaving is reduced to a subset of technical knowledge, dissociated from the embodied experience of the weaver and the collaborative networks of producers—weavers, designers, and traders. Also excluded from this narrative is the solidarity of the women weavers, who enable each other to do such difficult work that requires high levels of concentration while taking care of their domestic duties, child rearing, cooking, and caring for elders.

The association with the primitive also relegates carpet weaving to an older temporal order, one incapable of connecting to modern technologies.[27] Fortifying this view is the main argument advanced by connoisseur texts that the weavers follow tradition without understanding the design. E. Gans-Ruedin, an eminent connoisseur, writes:

> Indeed, the description of the motifs is as complete as possible, but it is often very difficult to obtain from the rug makers themselves the explanation of the designs; they use such and such motif in accordance with tradition, but they are no longer aware of its original meaning.[28]

Because the labor to produce the carpet is separated from its symbolic capital, the *savoir faire* becomes the natural function of traditional bodies. Through this move to detach the labor from the carpet's symbolic value, the commodity as fetish turns out to be the *raison d'être* of the symbolic production altogether.

Instructing the Eye and Domesticating the Carpet

According to the connoisseur texts, in order to appreciate a carpet and learn how to estimate its value, one needs to learn how to look at it and train the eye through aesthetic education backed by technical knowledge. As instructed in this quote form a carpet catalogue, "Merely glancing at an object does not enhance one's understanding of it. Only by looking again and again can one develop that degree of contemplation that leads to meditation and final involvement."[29] The more one partakes in connoisseurs' knowledge, the better one can appreciate the carpet and estimate its value. Alvin W. Pearson, a New Jersey-based carpet collector notes that "It takes a long time before you really get a feel for them, and it is a feel. It's almost like the stock market—not a mathematical science, unfortunately, but a matter of judgment."[30]

One of the important sites of Orientalia and the instruction of the eye was painting. Carpets became an important motif in Oriental painting in the seventeenth and eighteenth centuries. According to Delacroix they were the most beautiful pictures he had ever seen.[31] In Orientalist painting, the carpet is represented as either a luxury item and a component of aristocratic life or an exotic object displayed in Oriental markets. After the invention of the power loom in Europe, Kidderminster carpet weavers mimicked the famous Hunting Carpet, a cotton and silk masterpiece made by Ghyath ud-Din Jami under the Safavid dynasty in the sixteenth century.[32] The aspiration to own a Persian carpet was accompanied with the desire to produce it in Europe with new technological development. However, this desire was unfulfilled because of the cost of the labor in Europe and access to the cheap labor force in the colonies or

Figure 1.2 **Aesthetic Education of Children**
Heritage Images/Getty Images

semicolonies.[33] The drive to commodify this luxury item and make it affordable for the middle classes led to a short-lived attempt to produce it in Europe. Manufacturers soon shifted to a system based on the imperial export of raw materials to the Middle East, the exploitation of the cheap labor force in Iran and other parts of the Middle East and South Asia, and the import of the carpet to England, France, and Germany. The commodification of the luxury carpet also resulted in a distinction in terms of symbolic capital between the products of two kinds of labor: those produced for consumption in the public sphere by power looms in Europe and those that were imported mostly for domestic use.

A focus on the visual education of the eye as part of the connoisseurs' culture was crucial in the spectacularization of Orientalia and commercial capitalism. As Richards argues, the Great Exhibition of 1851 was crucial, for it is where "spectacle and capitalism became indivisible, a world produced, a world

distributed, a world consumed, a world still too much with us."[34] In connoisseur books, the reader or the viewer is called upon to learn about a scientific
mode of viewing, which is defined by modern modes of differentiation into
binaries such as nature/culture, tradition/modernity, primitive/civilized, East/
West, and women/men. The connoisseur's intervention becomes a necessity
for understanding the carpet, not just for Westerners but also for "Orientals"
because they, too, need to learn how to understand and appreciate the carpet.
According to Fernand Windels, a French carpet connoisseur,

> The Oriental does not make a green or blue carpet because these colors
> please him, but because they represent specific ideas that need to be
> recalled in the circumstance or the place where the finished work is to
> be used. Again, an Oriental carpet is read, it cannot be judged in the
> Occidental manner, one needs to be initiated to understand it and to
> appreciate it.[35]

Here Windels characterizes the "Oriental" as lacking the ability to make an aesthetic judgment. Highlighting the commodity while deskilling the labor is part
and parcel of this literature.

It is through the representation of the Persian carpet as an otherness domes-
ticated and displayed in the private sphere as a commodity that the site of the
European home becomes a unit of consumption rather than production. In
René Huyghes' view,

> it is in the art of the carpet that the Orient has developed the sense of the
> curve and the spiral, given so much prominence, which contrasts or com-
> plements the Occident. This opposition reveals a fundamental division of
> the history of forms, linked to civilizations: agrarian peoples, who are at
> the origin of the Occident, and nomadic peoples, who are at the origin
> of the Orient.[36]

In this passage, the carpet stands as a marker of a radical civilizational divide
between agrarian and tribal societies; this divide is neatly mapped onto the
East/West binary underpinning connoisseur discourse.

Although novelty is crucial for consumerism, I believe Orientalia created a
form of consumerism involving minimal need for innovation: one that relied
on a history of a highly mobile object, such as the Oriental carpet, that is fixed
in time and space. In an age where innovation is key to both production and
consumption, such a historical narrative enables the production and reproduction of Oriental carpets without a concomitant need to "make it new."

Indeed, the circulation of the carpets to Western markets was based on mass production, which relied on the repetition of the same design. However, since the carpet was introduced to the Euro-American consumer as an Oriental/Islamic art object, Western desire for it was steeped in and informed by a discourse of connoisseurship and "taste."

Accordingly, the carpet also becomes a site of differentiation between the taste of "Orientals" and the taste of Westerners. Coxon writes:

> Oriental carpets, in their evenly distributed colouring, all in quiet and subdued harmony, are a relief to the eye that has been exposed to the brilliant glare of the sunny East, and this probably accounts for the successful blending of colour peculiar to the Asiatic. An attempt has been made to introduce into the industries brighter and harsher colour to suit Western taste and a duller climate. But this was calculated to impair the Oriental theory of harmony of colour, and destroy the designs; it is, therefore, satisfactory to learn that the present Shah, Nasr Eddin, has forbidden the importation of foreign wools and dyes, and ordered that all carpets manufactured in his dominions must be made in the old recognized Persian patterns, free from European designs.[37]

In this text, the question of design and its transformation is defined in terms of geographic differences, causing both desire for change and a resistance to innovation. The climate and geographic area are collapsed within the framework of enlightened modernity; the Western desire for innovation is opposed to seeming resistance to new designs shown, in this case by the Oriental monarch of the Qajar dynasty. As order is at the center of modern everyday life, the middle and upper classes in the West want carpets with geometrical designs and cosmic plates as the mobile site of Asiatic harmony. The circularity of life displayed in these carpets promises to cosmopolitan consumers the idea of unity with a primordial past. The carpet, then, inhabited a liminal position somewhere between art, commodity, and craft. The ambiguous position of the carpet persists to this day, rendering it resistant to modern forms of artistic differentiation.

Oriental carpets, once described as luxury objects covering palaces and mosques, became an element of the bourgeois household in European private spaces in the twentieth century. With its extraordinary power to display the eternal beauty of nature, it makes the bourgeois home appear as an expansive as well as a cosmopolitan space, beyond the everyday world of labor and work. It is located within the temporality of *d'autrefois*, in Carl Hopf's terms, another time where "a sensibility of profound joy is awakened by a natural and healthy life that drew abundance and opened out in richness, force, and beauty."[38] In

this context, an art that is imagined to spring from natural development coun-
ters the anxieties surrounding industrialization and the putative dominance
of culture over nature. The carpet, when identified as emerging from the "the
inner abilities of Orientals," serves to assure the Occidentals about their own
modernity and internal ability for progress.[39] As William Morris notes, "To us
pattern-designers, Persia has become a holy land, for there in the process of
time our art was perfected."[40]

The idea of the home as the Other of the market creates a new site for the
consumption of particular commodities, including the Oriental carpet. In one
of the earliest books on the carpet, we read: "Home without a carpet is not
a home. Peace, intimacy, and forgetfulness of the outer world are impossible
without the absolute and complete absence of intruding sounds," and "Carpets
are essential to the man who thinks, to the woman who loves—and to the child
who falls."[41]

The Blood Bond of Transnational Masculinity

Connoisseur books complement the masculinized and masculinist politics of
mediation, as seen in a number of areas. Oriental carpets are described in gendered terms by Sydney Humphries. He writes, "The true Oriental carpet is vig-
orous, robust, and of fine-bred strength in texture, design, and coloring, and
can claim in all its essential characteristics to be thoroughly masculine."[42] Given
that most of those who mediate the process of carpet circulation are men, the

CARPET DEALING DIRECT WITH NATIVES. THE AUTHOR BARGAINING OVER A PRAYER CARPET IN DAGHESTAN.
TEMPERATURE 125 DEGREES.

Figure 1.3 **The connoisseur and the traders**
Herbert Coxon, *Oriental Carpets* (1884)

imagined audience of the connoisseur books is described in terms of masculinity. The carpet is mostly associated with private property, which is aesthetically appreciated and owned by men. Many carpet ads or images such as figure 1.3 depict the exchange of the carpet between local traders and European connoisseurs portraying men as subjects of trade. The most common visual representation of the carpet, a woman seated on it, associates the carpet with private property and women. Both the carpet and women are depicted as objects of the gaze rather than its subjects.

In an example of masculinized mediation, Sydney Humphries a connoisseur and collector of Oriental carpets, claims that women have no knowledge of home decoration. He writes:

> I am doing a good turn to my own sex in writing in this strain, and I offer no apologies to the fair sex: there is the danger of every woman being infected by the prevalent "suffragette" microbe, and of becoming persuaded that she really knows something about housekeeping—save the mark! The French superiority in matters domestic may be owing to the fact that the French housemaid is a "man," with his own sex, which forms the connecting-link with the Oriental, who from the beginning of things knew how to construct a fabric, which his sense of fitness and justice later taught him to appreciate and understand as the prime minister to his comfort and ease.[43]

Another early carpet connoisseur and trader, Herbert Coxon, in his travelogue *Oriental Carpets: How They Are Made and Conveyed to Europe* (1884), calls upon a masculinity that is defined by the imperial culture of travel, adventure, and trade. At the closing of his book, which could be considered one the earliest connoisseur books, he writes:

> On this account, I think I have demonstrated that my journey has been a successful one, and if nothing more, it should prove that provincial firms in England may emancipate themselves of the metropolis, and obtain their wares first hand from the East.[44]

While the carpet becomes a site of ultimate cultural and religious difference between the East and the West, Coxon depicts Oriental masculinity as benefiting from the weaving skills of wives, concubines, and slaves. Here Oriental and Persian women become a natural labor force, eternally sustaining the production of carpets, and men are the natural beneficiary of their work. He writes:

> The Mohamedan law allows a man four wives, but he can take as many concubines and slaves as the length of his purse will allow. The women are

largely employed in carpet making, chiefly confining themselves in Persia to the sizes that would come under our definition of a rug. The larger sizes are made by men. Almost all well-known embroideries of Persia are the work of the women of the harem. In the East, as the reader is probably aware, it is the women who mostly toil, while their lords indulge in the sublime pleasure of doing nothing.[45]

In this early observation about cultural difference, gender is constructed as a category transcending ethnic, class, and urban/rural differences. In this context, all Muslim men indulge in the pleasure of taking advantage of the women of their harem. For example, for Windels, this gender division mirrors the natural division of labor in Oriental societies. He writes, "For centuries the production of Oriental carpets was family-based. Women took care of weaving while men collected natural dye products."[46] Such a depiction of the Orient is very much consistent with gendered notions of Orientalism. As argued by Anne McClintock, "Knowledge of the unknown world was mapped as a metaphysics of gender violence—not as the expanded recognition of cultural difference— and was violated by the new Enlightenment logic of private property and possessive individualism."[47]

Gradually, this type of observation is replaced with the naturalization of the cheap labor force of women and children in the so-called East and its justified exploitation in the empire's new international division of labor. H. J. Whigman, author of *The Persian Problem* (1903), cites the (nonexistent) cost of women's labor as a reason the carpets are made in Persia under European supervision rather than in Europe:

> Fortunately for the British and American householders, the Persian woman is still a slave. If ever she is emancipated or raised out of the Mohammedan abyss to a higher level in the scale of existence Persian carpets will become a thing of the past.[48]

The exploitation of Persian women in the carpet industry was not only blamed on their religion but also cathected as beneficial for the consumptive production of British and US imperialism.

Subsumption or Sublime

The carpet's ability to express, among other things, the possibility of community, collaboration, and a form of territorialization that does not need to be attached to a defined national territory (other than the imaginary landscape of plants, animals, sky, clouds, and colors) becomes a threat to the humanist subject of connoisseur books. That subject is defined by the cultural values of an enlightened and civilized West, which is radically distinguished from the not-yet-civilized culture of the East. This potential for the territorialization of space conceals and defers the anxieties of cultural and artistic singularities that may interrupt and induce a new relation to desire, a relation that would create more perplexity than yearning in the interests of the imperial powers. The discourse of nationalism, which creates feelings of connection to and ownership of "there," exploits this potential for territorialization, while the discourses of old and neo-Orientalism and self-Orientalization, which create an exotic landscape that is domesticated and brought "here," do as well.[49] In other words, Orientalism made the carpets into exotic landscapes to be brought back to the heart of the empire, and nationalism made the carpets into a mobile territory to be consumed both in the homeland and in the diaspora. Both systems use the affective economy to produce value, to construct identities, and to generate a desire for consumption.

As I have elaborated in this chapter, both the subject figure produced in the connoisseur books as well as the subject/viewer who is constituted by these discursive practices are located within a scopic economy. This scopic economy links colonial exceptionalism with masculinist consumerism as it brings national and transnational spaces together by creating pedagogic and affective relations to material objects that are targeted to display total mastery of the Other's culture. In this process, the figure of the Other, feminized and rendered abject as an extension of nature as opposed to culture, is used to mediate such transnational encounters, to rationalize and legitimize the mastery of the knowledge-producing subjects over the process of subject formation. In other words, this process of subject formation cannot be separated from the practices of knowledge. Connoisseur books bring the power of science and money into conversation with the power of lifestyle values through the abstraction of the commodity. Such mediation brought various cultures into the same temporal and spatial framework through the vision and perspective of expert knowledge of a particular kind—in the case of connoisseurship, with the power to abstract the commodity from the conditions of its existence and the economy of needs.

Notes

1. On intertexuality, see Stuart Hall, *Representation: Cultural Representations and Signifying Practices* (London: Sage Publications, 1997), 232.
2. I expand on the concept and commodification of Orientalia in the following chapter.
3. Sarah B. Sherrill, "America and the Oriental Carpet: Seventeenth and Eighteenth Centuries," in *The Warp and Weft of Islam: Oriental Carpets and Weaving From Pacific Collections* (Seattle: Henry Art Gallery, 1978).

4. Barbara Maria Stafford, "Presuming Images and Consuming Words: The Visualization of Knowledge From the Enlightenment to Post-Modernism," in *Consumption and the World of Goods*, eds. John Brewer and R. Porter (New York and London: Routledge, 1994), 462–477.

5. According to Price, the idea of connoisseurship brings to mind the image of an educated and well-dressed gentleman with great taste. The antithesis of this image is the typical savage that is a scruffy, and not adequately educated with lascivious behavior. In her view "These two distant members of the human race occasionally come into contact through the market in Primitive Art, which one produces and the other assesses." Sally Price, *Primitive Art in Civilized Places* (Chicago: The University of Chicago Press, 1989), 7.

6. Ibid., 463–464.

7. Roland Barthes, *Critical Essays* (Evanston, IL: Northwestern University Press, 1972), 6. Also, Onno Ydema notes that a survey of pictorial sources from the Netherlands between the years of 1540 and 1700 relating to the study of Oriental carpets has resulted in the cataloguing of about 960 representations. See Onno Ydema, *Carpets and Their Datings in Netherlandish Paintings 1540–1700* (Netherlands: Walburg Pers, 1991), 123.

8. Edward Said, *Orientalism* (New York: Vintage Books, 1979), 176–177.

9. Mark Crinson cited in Mona Domash, *American Commodities in an Age of Empire* (New York: Routledge, 2006), 3.

10. Carol Bier, *Woven From the Soul, Spun From the Heart: Textile Arts of Safavid and Qajar Iran, 16th–19th Centuries* (Washington, DC: Textile Museum, 1987), 254.

11. Brewer and Porter refer to these concepts to talk about the impact of the new communication technologies on the distribution of objects. "Introduction," *Consumption and the World of Goods*, 6.

12. Cited in Peter Pels, "The Spirit of Matter: On Fetish, Rarity, Fact and Fancy," in *Border Fetishisms: Material Objects in Unstable Spaces*, ed. Patricia Spyer (New York and London: Routledge, 1998), 99–100.

13. Ibid., 102.

14. Said, *Orientalism*, 2.

15. Ibid., 1.

16. Bruno Latour, *Science in Action* (Cambridge, MA: Harvard University Press, 1987), 220.

17. See Inderpal Grewal, *Transnational America: Feminisms, Diasporas, Neoliberalisms* (Durham, NC: Duke University Press, 2005), 200.

18. Herr R. G. Hubel exhibition catalogue, *Oriental Carpets* (Liverpool, no date).

19. C. J. Delabère May, *How to Identify Persian Rugs: A Text-Book for Collectors and Students.* (London: G. Bell and Sons, 1920), 107.

20. John Gregorian, *Oriental Rugs of the Silk Route. Culture, Process, and Selection* (New York: Rizzoli, 2000), 151.

21. Rugs Direct website, "Tips on Decorating with Persian Rugs," Winchester, VA, www.rugs-direct.com/popularthemes/persianrugs.htm.

22. David Sylvester, "On Western Attitudes to Eastern Carpets," *Islamic Carpets From the Joseph V. McMullan Collection* (1972), 4, 6.

23. M. K. Zephyr Amir, *Supreme Persian Carpets* (Singapore: Tien Wah Press, 1972).

24. Cecil Arthur Edwards. *The Persian Carpet: A Survey of the Carpet-Weaving Industry of Persia* (London: Duckworth, 1960), i.

25. Nicolas Fokker, *Persian and Other Oriental Carpets for Today* (London: Lewis, Allen and Unwin, 1973).

26. C. R. Clifford, *Rugs of the Orient* (New York: Clifford & Lawton, 1911), 71.

27. As Essinger notes, there was definitely a crucial link between the Jacquard loom and the analytical engine invented by Babbage. See James Essinger, *Jacquard's Web: How a Hand Loom Led to the Birth of the Information Age* (Oxford, UK: Oxford University Press, 2004), 138.

28. E. Gans-Ruedin, *The Great Book of Oriental Carpets* (New York: Harper and Row, 1983), 7.

29. No source given. From the catalogue of the Herr R. G. Hubel exhibition, *Oriental Carpets*, Liverpool: Ashmolean Library, no date.

30. Cited in "Flying High in Magic Carpets," *Fortune*, May 1968, 165.

31. Cited from D. Sylvester in *Islamic Carpets from the Joseph V. McMullan Collection*, 4, 6, 10.

32. The Hunting Carpet was later sold to the Victoria and Albert Museum by a British broker on the advice of William Morris, the prominent English textile designer and artist. It depicts a hunting scene with real and phantasmatic animals, and is currently housed at the Museo Poldi Pezzoli, Milan.

33. "Souvenir Brochure to Commemorate the Visit of the Duke of York," Kidderminster, England, July 21, 1926.

34. Thomas Richards, *The Commodity Culture of Victorian England: Advertising and Spectacle 1851–1914* (Stanford, CA: Stanford University Press, 1990), 16.

35. Fernand Windels, *Le Tapis. Un Art-Une Industrie* (Paris: Les éditions D'antin, 1935), 144.

36. René Huyghes, *Tapis. Présent De L'orient a L'occident* (Paris: Institut du monde Arabe). Exposition associée au project de l'UNESCO "Routes de la Soie: Routes de la Dialogue" (1989), 7.

37. Herbert Coxon, *Oriental Carpets: How They Are Made and Conveyed to Europe* (London: T. Fisher Unwin, 1884), 56–57.

38. Carl Hopf, *Oriental Carpets and Rugs* (London: Thames and Hudson, 1913), 32.

39. Ibid., 34.

40. William Morris quoted in John Sweetman, *The Oriental Obsession: Islamic Inspiration in British and American Art and Architecture, 1500–1920* (Cambridge: Cambridge University Press, 1991), 178.

41. No author, *The Carpet Book* (London: Waring and Gillow, 1910), 3.

42. Sydney Humphries, *Oriental Carpets, Runners and Rugs and Some Jacquard Reproductions* (London: Adam and Charles Black, 1910), 293.

43. Ibid., 232.

44. Coxon, *Oriental Carpets*, 74.

45. Ibid., 55.

46. Windels, *Le Tapis. Un Art-Une Industrie*, 137.

47. Anne McClintock, *Imperial Leather, Race, Gender and Sexuality in the Colonial Contest* (New York and London: Routledge, 1995), 23.

48. Cited in Minoo Moallem, *Between Warrior Brother and Veiled Sister. Islamic Fundamentalism and the Politics of Patriarchy* (Berkeley: University of California Press, 2005), 46.

49. According to Ali Behdad, "Orientalist perceptions of the region continue to inform contemporary cultural practices in the West, while attempting to broaden the implications of his (Said) theory of otherness by attending to the ways in which neo-Orientalism produces distinctive discourses of alterity." Ali Behdad, *Camera Orientalis. Reflections on Photography of the Middle East* (Chicago and London: University of Chicago Press, 2016), 168.

2

TRANSNATIONAL ORIENTALIA AND CIVILIZATIONAL COMMODITIES

René Vincent :
Publicité pour le Printemps, 1907
Photo © Kharbine - Topabor

Figure 2.1 **An Old Carpet Ad from le Printemps**
© Kharbine-Tapabor

Anna Reeve Aldrich, an American poet (1866–1892), writes[1]

> Made Smooth some centuries ago
> By praying Eastern devotees,
> Blurred by those dusky nameless feet,
> And somewhat worn by shuffling knees
> In Ispahan [Isfahan]

It lies upon my modern floor,
And no one prays there anymore.

The Persian prayer carpet of Anna Reeve Aldrich's poem embodies the contradictions of modern consumerism both as a domesticated commodity brought
home from another culture as well as an obstacle to commodity exchange
because of its sacred objecthood and enigmatic power.[2] Persian carpets as commodities are part of a chain of goods called *Orientalia*. Orientalia include any
material object attributed to what is referred to as *Muhammadan, Musulman,
Oriental,* and *Persian* in nineteenth- and twentieth-century European and American writings. In this time period, Orientalia emerged as a significant part of
consumer culture. Orientalia brought the cultural and religious difference of
Eastern people to the heart of the empire. They epitomized consumer capitalism, neoliberal political economy, and the otherness within bourgeois subjects.
Orientalia included anything from jewelry to home furnishings to carpets. As
I demonstrated in the first chapter, expert knowledge of the so-called Orient
was crucial in educating and instructing people in Europe about the cultures
and arts of the Other. Oriental things became an attractive part of consumerism.[3] However, European modernity considered the culture and the art of the
Other to be collectible, belonging to the timeless temporality of the traditional
or the past as essence. Here essentialist notions of time converged with essentialist notions of culture to produce an Other located outside history.

Although there is a significant body of literature on Orientalism, there is
less work on material objects and their significance in the context of colonial
modernity, regarding not only consumption but also imaginary tropes (i.e., scientific or everyday images that inspired modern technologies). Antique and
rare objects, including the oldest carpets in the world, categorized as belonging to "Islamic civilization" represent an Oriental prehistorical age outside the
frame of modern circulation. In this chapter, I discuss how Oriental rugs as
mass-produced commodities became an important part of middle-class home
furnishings in twentieth-century Europe and the United States. Owning Oriental carpets was a signifier of wealth, travel, taste, and an appreciation for
primitive beauty.

Orientalia represented objects and things from the mystery land of the Orient. The material objects from the Orient complemented the spectacle of the
Other as objective and material. The nature/culture dichotomy was one of the
hegemonic and dominant ideologies in European modernity. Thomas Kim
notes that "Oriental objects construct an apolitical, ahistorical, and even immaterial knowledge of the Orient that simultaneously produces contradictions
with the political, historical, and material conditions of the Far East and Asians

in America."[4] He goes on to argue that the aestheticization of the Orient provided space for the West to exercise authority over the Other, especially in contact zones. However, I argue that the appeal of Oriental carpets is also linked to the history of exploitation of cheap manual labor in the form of exposing, abjectifying, and rejecting the ordeal. I believe that what Thomas Kim calls the "aesthetic production of the Far East,"[5] and in this case "the Oriental," is more than consumption of the Orient by the West; it is also the production of the Orient as a series of commodities. In this context, the empire of merchandise along with the aestheticization of the Orient play a crucial role in holding together the net and the work. In other words, as probed by Samuel Weber, "what holds networks together?"[6] Affects are central to the aestheticization and distribution of sensible in the sense of something that affects someone, not in terms of emotions and feelings but something dynamic and something that comes from elsewhere. Affect is defined as "a force or forces of encounter,"[7] the capacity to affect or to be affected. Jacques Rancière refers to the "distribution of the sensible," to recognize where sensation takes place in relation to what aesthetic transformation encompasses.[8] According to Samuel Weber, "an affect, unlike a feeling, can never be understood as the exclusive property of an isolated individual since its origin lies elsewhere."[9] Rey Chow notes that Walter Benjamin's work is so powerful precisely because he considers collecting and the love of things as a form of historical materialist practice.[10]

In this chapter, I trace how Orientalist narratives and imaginaries invested value in carpets and put them into circulation. I argue that the discourse on Orientalia in general and Persian carpets in particular produces value, regulates labor, and channels desire through consumerism. An interrogation of cultural representations in this context is crucial because representational practices glue together an economy of affects with political economy, binding empire and nation as well as labor and capital. In other words, Orientalia as a series of commodities links consumptive production with productive consumption through an economy of affects.[11] In the empire, the sentimental attachment to the carpet took place in the collection, possession, and exchange of a domesticated object, an object produced by "people who don't know or appreciate it" (as stated by some carpet connoisseurs).[12] Academic work on the Victorian novel has shed some light on sentimentalized objects and their meanings in stories.[13] For example, Deborah Cohen describes the Victorians as "the first people to be so closely identified with their belongings," arguing that "these belongings come to seem dually endowed: they are at once products of a cash market and, potentially, the rare fruits of a highly sentimentalized realm of value both domestic and spiritual, a domain defined by being anything but marketable."[14] We still need to understand how an affective economy keeps certain commodities in circulation while maintaining and perpetuating uneven relations of power in the postcolonial era.

Orientalia as both commodities and moving images emerged as the result of encounters between European colonialism and Middle Eastern and North African societies and cultures. These liminal sites of encounters created space for an affective force that was put into action and oriented toward consumerism. While Oriental carpets as objects exhibited hybridity and mélange resulting from centuries of cultural borrowing and cultural exchange, colonial modernity's construction of the carpets as a site of Oriental otherness changed the situation. The modern episteme relied on the polarization of modern and traditional, Occidental and Oriental, and civilized and primitive by using totalizing ordering regimes based on hierarchies of class, race, gender, and nation.

Orientalia as Civilizational Commodities

The seminal work of Edward Said on Orientalism has undoubtedly generated a world of scholarship, including a substantial body of work on various forms of Orientalism. However, we are still far from understanding the relationship between Orientalia and Orientalism. This gap resulted theoretically not only from the Enlightenment investment in the concept of the human as separate from everything else—especially from cultures fetishized as "primitive"—but also from the separation of material culture from systems of representation. Orientalism, as noted by Adam Geczy, "nourished the illusion that somewhere within it, if one looked and preserved hard enough, there was the possibility of a return to a primitive truth." (Adam Geczy, *Fashion and Orientalism* (London: Bloomsbury, 2013), 156.) Indeed, Orientalism is relevant to not only the carpet as a sign, a trope, or an image but also the carpet as a material object. As material objects, Oriental carpets are boundary objects separating the East and the West, domesticating the East and subordinating it to the spaces of consumerism in the West. Indeed, owning material objects implies more than an investment in the image of the carpet or the trope of the carpet.

The representation of commodities in world fairs, exhibitions, and museums in addition to their circulation through trade have been crucial to both colonial and postcolonial formations. Nevertheless, scholarship has rarely focused on commodities. Discussions of the production of the "Orient" itself as a commodity are frequent in the literature. However, Orientalia and Orientalized commodities, including carpets, have not been objects of scholarly attention. Bringing questions of representation into conversation with issues of commodity circulation in this chapter, I first show that the discourse on Orientalia is not secondary but central to the process in which these commodities are produced and consumed. More specifically, Orientalism as a colonial and neocolonial discourse is put into action through material culture and commodities. In other words, the deployment of commodities has been crucial to the constitution and maintenance of a cultural hierarchy and the semiotic distinction between the Orient and the Occident. Second, I discuss the Oriental carpets as *civiliza-tional commodities*, or commodities that served to characterize the Orient and Occident as opposing realms occupying different hierarchical positions in the civilizational ladder. As Baudrillard noted, that which opposed the Occident seemed to seduce it.[15] Third, through a few examples of stories, images, and sound samples, I illustrate how the economy of affects and an attachment to things Oriental functioned.

One of the important discursive implications of Orientalism has been related not only to the representation of the Orient but also to the ways in which this discourse actively Orientalizes the Other, as Hsu-Ming Teo has stated.[16] Part of this act of Orientalizing is to create not just a consumable Orient, as some schol-ars argue, but an Orient defined by commodities, an Orient that could either be brought back from the Middle East or North Africa or directly ordered for European and American consumption—a material Orient filled with commod-ities that match the exotic and magical primitivism of its peoples and cultures. Commodities with supernatural powers were considered an extension of the Oriental mysterious and irrational life, contrasting with the scientific world of ideas and the rationality of life in the West. As Madeleine Dobie demonstrates, as early as the late seventeenth and early eighteenth centuries, Orientalization was one of the processes that enabled colonial commodities to be integrated into French furniture culture.[17] Indeed, an integral part of both Orientalism and colonialism has been the establishment of trade routes between Europe and the United States and various locations in the Middle East and North Africa.

The discourse of Orientalism created a sense of temporal and spatial distance from people, contributing to the idea that the Orient was a land outside history. Orientalia brought what was kept at a distance into proximity, inviting sensual-ity, an Orient that could be domesticated, touched, smelled, and felt. Fetishism and romantic attachment to things foreign and exotic continue to mark peo-ple's material life on an everyday basis. Whereas some scholars refer to colonial commodities to talk about commodity circulation under colonial rule, I pro-pose the concept of *civilizational commodities* to describe how Orientalia were not only represented as exotic commodities coming from distant and mysterious lands, but they also constituted cultural distinctions and civilizational hierar-chies. In other words, civilizational commodities confirmed cultural and civi-lizational difference. Such goods maintained the boundaries between the East and the West, the Oriental and the Occidental, the primitive and the modern, and the religious and the secular, no matter their proximity to or distance from the observer. Also, as transnational commodities, Orientalia co-presented and linked disconnected social, cultural, and geopolitical locations, facilitating and rationalizing the establishment of an international gendered division of labor.

Orientalia were critical to what Foucault calls technologies of power that mediate the relationships between empire, nation, expert knowledge, and the self. Some scholars, including Veblen, Barthes, and Bourdieu, have shown how consumption is related to class and status distinction.[18] I further argue that consumption is also a marker of colonial and postcolonial power as well as a site of gendering and racialization in the geopolitical division of labor. The meanings of the Occident and the Orient are consistently managed not only through the symbolic and aesthetic boundaries of taste and style mapped onto social, cultural, and geopolitical boundaries but also through patterns of consumption.

As Georg Simmel notes, modernity destroyed pre-modern notions of people being bounded to a local community and replaced them with the separation of objects and subjects in the money economy.[19] He writes: "[T]he individual constructs his environment of variously stylized objects; by his doing the objects receive a new center, which is not located in any of them alone, but which they all manifest through the particular way they are united."[20] In my view, aesthetic stylization as part of an affective economy or an economy of affects resolved the tension between individual behavior and the broader generality of norms in colonial modernity. What I refer to as an affective economy is an economy that functioned both through an uneven international division of labor as well as through stories, images, and sounds. This economy functioned through networks lacking a single center and held together by the stories people told and the capacity to disseminate those stories, as Samuel Weber notes.[21] The contradictions and tensions between the subject positions in the net and the regulation of the net required a normative system sustained by various subjects, including laborers. Orientalia intervened in this process to unite the subject and the commodities surrounding one's daily life into a new whole. In other words, Orientalia created an assembled unity of specific commodities that entered or remained in the commodity chain due to the aesthetic stylization of consumerism.

To elaborate further on the Orientalization of Persian carpets, I go on to show how Orientalia became central to Orientalism as a discourse, constructing the Orient as a space that was portable and imaginary yet prone to domestication as part of home furnishings in contradistinction from the Occident. Carpets also created a readable and recognizable territory or an Orientalized nature. They also offered an artificial universe that could be domesticated and made into mobile property. Given the reliance of colonial modernity on the use of the laws of vision as well as optical devices, the Oriental carpet—both as an optical device and as a site of complex representational practices—became a vital mediating commodity.[22] To illustrate this process, I examine the representation of Orientalia in Orientalist films, advertisements (both printed and digital), and fiction.

World's Fairs and Museums

The discourse of Orientalism mediated the circulation of Persian carpets. Modern institutions, including world's fairs and museum exhibitions, facilitated this process. Also, as Jeffrey Auerbach notes, through the mediation of objects, remote territories became as much a part of the colonial world as home territories.[23] The Paris Expositions Universelles of 1873, 1889, 1900, and 1913 all included a "Pavillon du Perse" displaying items ranging from architecture to decorative art of Iran.[24] Persian carpets were recognized as the best pile carpets out of all the Oriental carpets. The well-known Hunting Carpet, mentioned in Chapter 1, was displayed at the Vienna Exhibition as early as 1891.[25]

According to Manya Ghazarian, the major exhibition in Vienna in 1891 was called "Oriental Decorative and Applied Arts." Based on this exhibition, Alois Riegl wrote his first work on Oriental carpets (this work is in German). Ghazarian also notes, "In 1910 there was an exhibition in Munich called 'Masterpieces of Mohammedan Art.' This exhibition included a section called Armenian carpets. The Persian carpets were represented as distinguished from Indian and Turkish carpet because of 'their refinement,' 'their imaginative garden and hunting scenes,' and 'their uninterrupted rhythm of line.'" According to art historian and museum director Wilhelm R. Valentiner,[26] many exhibitions in Europe and the United States were organized by Christian missionaries, such as "The Oriental in London" exhibition held at the Royal Agricultural Hall from June 4 to July 11, 1908.

The idea of progress was central to the politics of display in these international fairs and exhibitions. For example, in a series of articles published in July 1873 entitled "Textile Industry at the Vienna Exhibition," Dr. H. Groth describes Persian carpets as coming from

> the Eastern tribes—Persia, a state without any really perceptible progress, appears entirely enveloped in carpets and coverings; and no product, no manufacture, no industry of any kind whatever could justly be placed at the side of this branch of manufacture in the case of this primitive state.[27]

The representation of Persian carpets as products from a primitive state opened up space for the settlement of the European companies in Iran and their control over the carpet production there.

Most exhibits were constructed around the display of otherness and the idea of a division between nations—the advanced nations were contrasted with those nations that were eternally backward and beyond civilization. These exhibitions and fairs functioned as a spectacle of commodities displaying the idea of progress through material culture. The commodity spectacle became the visual expression of civilizational hierarchies, inviting consumers to purchase not only the value invested in the commodity but also the value endowed in the self as the subject of the gaze and on the side of progress. The spectacle concealed the subjects of labor; the cohesive idea of nation and its claim on the ownership of commodities displaced the labor into the realm of the invisible. The Persian carpet as a national fetish established the boundaries of we-ness and otherness and became the signifier of a nation unified, regardless of hierarchies of class, gender, and ethnicity that existed within the populace.

Gradually, transnational commodities became important parts of world exhibitions and were displayed in department stores in the early twentieth century. For example, the London Colonial and Indian Exhibition in 1886 and the annual Ideal Home Exhibition first held in London in 1908 were important sites of this spectacle, displaying commodities that fostered and articulated imperial and nationalistic notions of identity and culture.[28]

From the Cloud Carpet to the Flying Carpet

The material culture of Europe, including the domain of furniture and decoration, was profoundly influenced by the perception and representation of the Orient as a "static, unchanging environment, subject to despotic governance and unfavorable to business," in Madeleine Dobie's terms.[29] This form of representation included scientific and technological imaginings. For example, the trope of the flying carpet was central in the Orientalist imagination.

In January 1919, the *London Times* reported on one of a series of lectures arranged by the Royal Aeronautical Society. Addressing a large audience of children assembled in Central Hall, Westminster, the speaker invited them to Constantinople and India on what he described as the up-to-date magic carpet with the seven-leagued boots, which would take them to the places of their fairy tales.[30]

An article published the following year by the *Times*, entitled "In the Upper Air: Flying Over a Cloud Carpet," demonstrates the European imperial obsession with the aerial view, which Caren Kaplan describes as "the view from above the ground [that] inspires and creates some of the most powerful social relations of sight and knowledge in the European Enlightenment and its imperial and neoliberal aftermath."[31] The following quote from the *Times* in 1920 exposes this aerial vision:

Soon we are threading our way among slender white peaks of cloud standing like giant sentinels in a silent freezing world. . . . Low down on the right there, like a great gray beetle crawling across the pure white carpet, is seen the shadow of our own machine thrown by the sun's powerful rays. It is moving, of course, in a perfectly straight line and one which is parallel to our line of flight. It emphasizes the clouds' contours very definitely and is at last lost to sight as the machine begins to climb still lower and lower by scarcely perceptible degrees. Now we are soaring too high in the heavens to recognize the snatches of the earth which we occasionally glimpse through odd gaps in the cloud carpet. The bend of a river here, the corner of a thick wood there, flash into sight sometimes as we gaze vertically downward. But they are without identity to us; they serve only to recall the fact that the earth still exists, and they are perhaps not so much a charm of the present experience as harbingers of the time when we must descend to the world again.[32]

Down below, empty lands "without identity" are displayed for the imperial gaze. This view continues to be central to our militarized neocolonial and neoliberal world. For example, the term "carpet-bombing" is used to refer to unguided aerial bombing that damages every part of an area. This tactic, employed in World War II and the Vietnam War, has been frequently used by the United States since the occupation of Iraq and Afghanistan. As Marina Warner notes, "The flying vehicle grants superior powers—to see farther, to know and control more. More precisely, a carpet or rug miniaturizes the view, unfolding a full planar perspective plan with elevation included. The aerial view defies the laws of time and space."[33] The idea of a flying carpet creates space for imperial adventures, "adventures that transform a pilot from novice to journeyman and eventually, skilled aviator."[34]

The exotic flying carpet of the *Arabian Nights* has been crucial in the popular Western imagination. The art historian David Schorr refers to the flying rugs as "a common childhood dream."[35] A look through Western literary history reveals a fascination with, in Warner's words,

> the idea of flying—like birds, like angels—with angelic bodilessness, sexual delight, fairy ethereality, untrammelled motion, uplift and intoxication— and also with vertigo, disorientation, the unbearable lightness of being. It was a property of spirits and animals but also of alarming things, of 'the invisible worm, that flies in the night,' insects, dragons, devils.[36]

As an auratic object, the Oriental carpet was attached to the ideas of magic exploited extensively in Orientalist movies and imagery, including the image of the flying carpet both as a weapon of war as well as a virtual tourist trope. According to Kajri Jain, "auratic objecthood" refers to a mass-cultural form that demands a mode of analysis that can address the levels of signification mobilized by multiplicity, repetition, and circulation. Jain argues that auratic objecthood does not stem from authorial originality but performative practices in the realms of circulation and reception.[37] As a weapon of war, the carpet inspired the modern scientific and military imagination; the first airplanes were called "cloud carpets," and carpet-bombing has become an integral part of war technologies. The carpet was also invested with sacred power enabling spiritual and virtual voyages, as it was used in religious and everyday ceremonies. In colonial films from as early as 1926, documentaries such as *The Procession of the Sacred Carpets* displayed a European fascination with the ritualistic use of the carpet in Egypt.

There is a long tradition of Orientalist and neo-Orientalist painting depicting the flying carpet that continues to this day; this tradition includes illustrations for the *Arabian Nights* done by several artists since the early twentieth century. One of the oldest drawings of the Oriental flying carpet was created in 1913 by Edmund Dulac, who used the techniques of Persian miniature for his illustrations. French Orientalist Leon Carré's illustrations for the *Arabian Nights* in 1926, which are among the most sexualized versions, include multiple depictions of the Oriental flying carpet. More recently, painting and photography of the flying carpet influenced by cinematography and 3D art are relying on the iconography of an Orientalist imaginary.

Oriental carpets appeared in European paintings as part of bourgeois furniture, entered the bourgeois home as a commodity in the late nineteenth century, and became portable and mobile through Orientalist films.[38] Linking the class, race, and gender-based notions of respectability with the patterns of consumption, carpets as both image and material objects connected the private sphere with the public sphere, the interior with the exterior, and the home with the market. This process fostered modern notions of the self as separated from what was materially outside of it: the Oriental, the primitive, the Other. However, the Oriental carpet was not only displayed and represented in high art and museums; it also became an icon of popular culture.

The Magic of the Carpet

The magic carpet appeared in translations of Oriental tales in Europe, especially various translations and adaptations of what became the *Arabian Nights*, first in the eighteenth century and then in nineteenth century.[39] The image was followed by drawings, images, and filmic reproductions of this icon up to the present. Oriental carpets have been central in the construction of Orientalia as

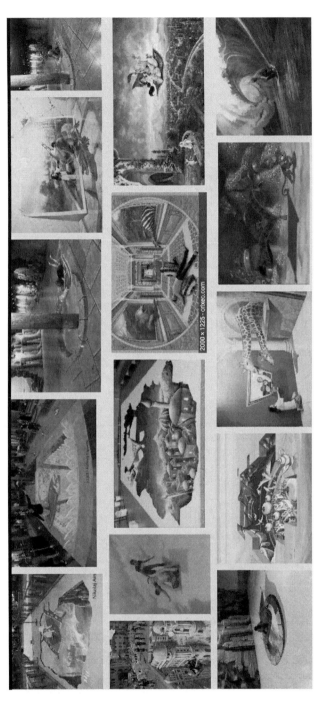

Figure 2.2 **Screenshot of various images of the flying carpets**

Figure 2.3 **Playing Magic Carpet**
© The Strong

a vital part of the spatial imagination of the Orient. Some commodities, such as rings, lamps, clothing items, and carpets, have been represented in stories as magical and talismanic objects with supernatural forces both positive and adverse. These objects represented a form of supernatural and irrational knowledge that was acquired in the non-Western world.

Sometimes appearing as a traveling bed with "coverlets and cushions," as in "The Tale of Ala Al-Din Abu Shamat," the flying carpets enabled the idea of speediness, of traveling in "less time than it takes to piss."[40] Also, the flying carpet enabled an aerial view that "defies the laws of time and space," in Marina Warner's words.[41] Their existence is forceful as they become commodities that can be domesticated and put under the decree of their owners.[42] Orientalist imagery, along with moving and digitalized images, bring such products from the realm of storytelling and imagination into the realm of everyday consumerism. In this context, Orientalia in general and carpets in particular become fetish objects that draw a border between the familiar and the exotic as well as the ordinary and the uncanny, the latter overcoming distance, domesticating and repressing the memory of colonialism.

For example, the story "Three Princes and the Princess Nouronnihar" in *Arabian Nights* tells of a sultan of India who had three sons and a beautiful niece whom he raises in her palace after his brother's death. After realizing that all his sons have fallen in love with the princess, he sends them to three different countries, telling them that the one who brings back the most extraordinary and rare object could marry her. The first brother, Hussain, travels to the kingdom of Bisnagar in Gujrat; the second brother, Ali, goes to Persia; and the third brother, Ahmed, goes to Samarkand in central Asia. After visiting the exotics land of India, Persia, and Samarkand and exploring their bazaars and *bezesteins* (covered bazaars for valuable things including jewelry, carpets, and clothes), Prince Hussain returns with a flying carpet, Prince Ali returns from Persia with an ivory tube through which he can see anything and anybody, and Prince Ahmed returns with a magic apple that can cure any sick person. Each was initially distrustful of the price and the magical quality of the merchandise they purchased. However, they realize that all the objects are necessary and complementary: the tube helps them find out that the princess is sick and on her death bed, the carpet helps them to get to her as fast as they can, and the apple cures the princess. The story constructs an Orient that stretches from India to Persia, Central Asia to China and Japan, with their mysterious bazaars and bezesteins as the primary sites of exchange of strange and extraordinary goods. It also depicts the patriarchal and heteronormative marriage as the state of nature. The flying carpet in this story can do magic but does not have a voice.

Today, many magazines and websites retell the stories of the *Arabian Nights* to promote consumer desire for the consumption of Oriental carpets. For example, Elizabeth Butcher's article, "How to Buy a Magic Carpet," published in the *Daily Mail* in November 2002, instructs the reader how to purchase carpets in Morocco. Obviously, the "magic carpet" in this context is a good quality carpet. Ultimately, the carpets start to be depicted as having a silent voice. On a website representing a store called The Magic Carpets in Nevada, we read: "Oriental rugs have enchanted and fascinated owners and viewers throughout the world for centuries. They are the embodiment of beauty, and when we open ourselves to their message and take delight in their exotic designs, we enrich our lives immeasurably."[43] In this context, the carpets are depicted as animating and passing messages to the consumers.

Comic books have also used the image of the flying carpet. The comic book, audiobook, music album, and video game "Asterix and the Magic Carpet"[44] uses numerous Orientalist tropes, including the magic carpet. The Persian carpet merchants' visual mass-culture glorification of an adventurous and masculine hero who travels to the exotic and Oriental lands via the magic carpet is central to many commodities.

Inanimate Animation

With the advent of the moving image, photography, and cinematography, films from genres ranging from animated cartoon to fiction to documentary constructed the Oriental carpet as magical, and carpet-producing countries such as Iran as mysterious places. In this context, the image of the carpet produces a series of material commodities beyond the Oriental carpet as such. This includes movies, TV series, cartoons, amusement park activities, dolls, computer games, and music videos and songs. I will elaborate on a few examples to illustrate these commodities.

Animated cartoons are among the very early examples of Orientalization of the Persian carpets.[45] One of the oldest depictions of the flying carpet and trade between the West and the Arab and Muslim worlds is a series of silent animations called "Felix the Cat" that was made in the United States in 1919 and was popular until 1928. The anthropomorphic and Eurocentric character of this animation was commercialized immediately and inspired the manufacturing of various goods including stuffed animals, toys, and postcards at a time when Oriental carpets started to enter the US market. In one episode called

Figure 2.4 **Screenshot 1 from Arabianics**

Figure 2.5 **Screenshot 2 from Arabianics**

"Arabianics," Felix the Cat comes across a hungry, foreign-looking vendor and exchanges his milk for an Oriental carpet. The carpet can fly and takes him to an architecturally Orientalized land and the bazaar, where he exchanges his carpet for a bag of jewelry. Soon a man discovers his bag of jewelry and steals it from him. Felix discovers that the man owns a group of women to whom he throws the stolen jewelry. Felix finally tricks the women into dancing and takes back the jewelry hidden under their clothing. This episode displays an Orient full of thieves and traders who own women, jewelry, and carpets.

It does not take long before the flying carpet of the *Arabian Nights* is transformed from an inanimate object with magical powers to an animated commodity with the power to speak and to act on its own behalf. The Disney culture industry has extensively capitalized on the trope of the Oriental flying carpet to sell movies, amusement park activities, and consumer goods. Disney's magic carpet was made for the well-known animated film *Aladdin* (1992). As described by Disney Wikia, "it is a sentient Persian carpet . . . one of the first computer-animated characters in a feature film . . . to possess an almost human level of intelligence."[46] The magic of the Disney Persian carpet is that it helps Princess Jasmine and Aladdin to fall in love with each other. In these and similar representations, carpets as commodities animate, talk, transform, move, and improvise.

The Disney industry has created numerous commodities for many animated films including *The Princess and the Frog* and *The Lion King*, a number of TV series, and various video games. Disney has also created a flying-carpet aerial carousel ride, featured in several of its amusement parks and resorts in Tokyo, Paris, and Shanghai. Numerous small commodities and toys have been produced around the Disney narrative of the flying carpet. The Aladdin and Jasmine dolls made by Disney come in different collections with prices ranging from $29 to $500. Many other companies have reproduced these dolls, including Fisher-Price. Orientalized dolls are a hodgepodge bundle of signifiers borrowed from different cultures. They mainly remain a morphed version of Barbie and Ken dolls. The clear messages of these products, which target consumers of all ages and social classes including children, are the fixing of gender and racial boundaries and the promotion of heteronormative romance through the possession of commodities.[47]

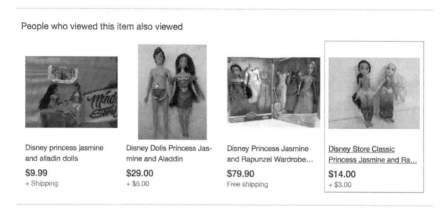

People who viewed this item also viewed

| Disney princess jasmine and alladin dolls | Disney Dolls Princess Jasmine and Aladdin | Disney Princess Jasmine and Rapunzel Wardrobe… | Disney Store Classic Princess Jasmine and Ra… |
| $9.99 + Shipping | $29.00 + $5.00 | $79.90 Free shipping | $14.00 + $3.00 |

Figure 2.6 **Screenshot of Dolls**

Figure 2.7 **Gendered Pleasures of Riding a Magic Carpet**
dimj/Shutterstock.com

In this context, not only have representational practices been crucial in the circulation of carpets but the interference of specific media, especially print and visual media and films, has been vital in the mobilization of new meanings and values attached to such commodities in the marketplace. Hence, the intervention of media technologies, especially films, not only functioned as a supplement to capitalism and its value system but also produced new value for the empire and later for the nation and its diaspora. In this context, Oriental carpets could be characterized as fetish objects in the sense that they depict the primitivism of the Other, concealing relations of production geopolitically and also assigning a magical and cultish character to Oriental societies.

A number of the old and neo-Orientalist feature movies use the trope of the flying Oriental carpet as part of a whole series of commodities (bottles, lamps, crystals, jewelry, etc.) to construct the materiality of the Orient as a land of violent masculinities, submissive femininities, and uncanny commodities, a territory crowded with irrational subjects and mysterious objects. Some examples of these movies in the United States are *The Thief of Baghdad*, directed by Raoul Walsh, 1924; *The Magic Carpet*, written by David Mathews and directed by Lew Landers, 1951; *The Arabian Adventure*, directed by Kevin Connor, 1979; and *The Phoenix and the Magic Carpet* (based on a fantasy novel for children by Edith Nesbit, first published in 1904), directed by Zoran Perisic, 1995.

The Thief of Baghdad is the first feature Hollywood film where the Persian magic carpet makes its appearance.[48] The screenplay assembles several stories from the *Arabian Nights* and creates its own version of an Orientalist fantasy combining violence, romance, and magic, all taking place in the remote land of Baghdad. The film is silent but coupled with intertitles and captions. Caliph Ali, who rules Baghdad, has a daughter called Princess Amina. It is time for the princess to get married and the condition for the suitors is that the one who brings the most extraordinary object "will win her." The main hero is Karim, the thief of Baghdad who steals whatever he wishes but helps the poor. However, he starts to change as soon as he falls in love with Princess Amina. To qualify to marry the princess, he has to risk his life to get through seven dangerous gates from which no one has returned. At the end of his journey, Karim finds a winged horse and a few magical objects that enable him to come back to the palace. In the meantime, the other suitors find rare treasures. The magic rug appears in the movie when Sultan of Persia goes to the Shiraz bazaar to look for a treasure. The carpet is the only commodity exchanged in the market. While the carpet looks like any other, the secret is that it is magical and can fly. In the end, the Sultan of Persia brings the flying carpet from Shiraz; the Prince of Indies brings a magic crystal through which one can see everything from an ancient site in what is referred in the movie as "Kandehar," and the Mogul Prince from Asia

Figure 2.8 The Thief of Baghdad 1
Screenshot 1, Douglas Fairbanks, *The Thief of Baghdad*, Directed by Raoul Walsh, 1924

Figure 2.9 The Thief of Baghdad 2
Screenshot 2, Douglas Fairbanks, *The Thief of Baghdad*, Directed by Raoul Walsh, 1924

brings a golden apple with the capacity to bring the dead to life.[49] The Mogul Prince plans to poison the princess and use the golden apple to give her life back, thus winning the competition. Karim returns to the palace on the flying horse and saves the princess from the suitors by flying her up to the moon. The carpet is depicted as a mobile commodity, not merely an object bought and sold in the Shiraz market but also a moving site of heterosexual romance.

Another neo-Orientalist movie using the flying carpet trope is *The Magic Carpet* starring Lucille Ball. In depicting the Orient as the radical opposite of the Occident, the film creates a mishmash of incongruities. The Oriental characters are portrayed by white cast members dressed up in a rather strange mixture of Indian sari and belly dancing costume, with transparent veils for women and peculiar turbans for men. The dance music in the film is Iranian, while the dancers are supposedly performing Egyptian belly dance (a rather peculiar kind of music and dance is performed in all these movies).

The film opens with a scene of a bazaar full of Persian carpets somewhere in the Orient and tells the story of a caliph called Omar who becomes subject to the conspiracy of his rival Ali. Before dying, he asks his wife, Queen Yazmina, to use his flying carpet to save the baby boy. Before she is killed, the queen puts the baby on the carpet and hangs the caliph's necklace around his neck. The carpet flies and lands at the door of Ahkmid, his uncle, who is a physician and a pharmacist. Ahkmid removes the collar and raises Ramoth to become a young doctor who rises against the Caliph Ali's tyranny without knowing that he is the real heir to the throne.

In addition to film depicting Oriental difference through harems, bazaars, clothes, carpets, and desert, the film constructs the Oriental subjects as despotic and patriarchal. The women in the Caliph's harem are portrayed as obsessed with sex, men, and their beautification during the day as they wait for the night to satisfy men's desires. Similar to the Arabianics cartoon, women are obsessed with jewelry when it is thrown at them. The one exception to the film's depiction of women as wives, concubines, dancers, and servants is Lida, the sister of Ramoth's friend Razi, who is a tomboy at the beginning of the movie. However, Lida becomes domesticated at the end of the film when Ramoth finally becomes the Caliph, marries her, and takes her to fly with him on the magic carpet to see the world. In the last scene on the carpet, Ramoth calls Lida a tigress, and she responds, "From now on you see a lamb."

The carpet symbolizes the Orient, and as an object appears everywhere: at the bazaar, at the physician's house, at the palace. In addition, its magical powers enable it to play a central role in the film's action. The magic carpet is intelligent and knows what to do once the secret code is spelled out. It is also a military tool; its speed and flying ability enable Ramoth to use aerial vision

Figure 2.10 The Magic Carpet Screenshot 1
The Magic Carpet, directed by Lew Landers, Katzman Corporation, 1951

Figure 2.11 The Magic Carpet Screenshot 2
The Magic Carpet, directed by Lew Landers, Katzman Corporation, 1951

to pour pepper on his enemies from the sky. The carpet is also able to resolve questions of mobility and transportation in Ramoth's military plans, and eventually saves Ramoth and his friend from beheading once they are arrested and jailed by the palace guards.

The film's depiction of subjects (women and slaves), clothing (veils, turbans, sexy outfits), landscape (desert, bazaar, palace, harem), objects (clothing, jewelry, and carpets), and power structures (patriarchy, despotism, tyranny, betrayal, and duplicity) represents the Orient and includes Egypt, Persia, Syria, Iraq, and Mecca. The juxtaposition of the landscape, the architecture, the gendered subjects—obedient, jealous, and deceitful women and belligerent and cruel men—the clothing, and the furniture (mostly carpets) creates the Orient as a fantasy world domesticated and brought to Hollywood for mass consumption.[50]

The stories around the flying carpet are perhaps some of the most important narratives of modernity; they display a desire for mobility, travel, romance, and exoticism. They also distort the linkage between production and consumption by turning consumption into an affective act "in time" and portraying production as belonging to the magic "out of time."

Diaspora

The image of the flying carpet continues to be in circulation in popular culture. It is even used by diasporic communities, including Iranians, as a self-Orientalizing trope to construct the culture of the homeland as being beyond time and space. For example, Payvand and the Iranian Federated Women's Club (IFWC), a diasporic community organization established in 1995–1996 in the San Francisco Bay Area, uses the trope of the magic carpet in the slogan on their website: "Imagine that you have your very own magic carpet."[51] In a short outreach film celebrating Nourouz (the Iranian new year), the image of the flying carpet returns to take the diasporic community back to the mythical time of Persia, or to the Eleventh Annual Iranian Arts and Cultural Festival in 2008.

Here is the translation of the opening of the film:

> Imagine that you have your very own magic carpet and that you have just asked the genie in the lamp to take you on a journey. You say you wish to travel through time, to an ancient and faraway place, and experience a rich culture. You say you wish to learn some of its history, about its kings and leaders, about its religions and rituals; you wish to get a glimpse into the lives of its beautiful women whose dark eyes reflect intelligence and determination; you wish to taste the rich flavors of its cuisine. "Your wish is my command!" says the unfailing genie. And the genie brings you to the perfect place: to the Payvand and Iranian Federated Women's Club (IFWC) Eleventh Annual Iranian Arts and Cultural Festival!

Here the flying carpet of the Western imagination provides a vantage point for diasporic Iranians as they reinvent themselves as inhabitants of a world beyond history. The flying carpet in this context stands again for a mythical past closing off the possibility of embodying one's cultural difference to be able to open it to a critical discourse. This time, a consumerist gaze operates through the self-disciplining and self-Orientalization of the diasporic communities to erase the subject position that remains beyond its control.

As this chapter has shown, representational practices were crucial in the circulation of Oriental carpets. The mediation of print, photography, and film mobilized new meanings, enabling the investment of new value into the carpet as a commodity. Actually, the intervention of media technologies, especially films, not only functioned as a supplement to capitalism and its value system but also produced new value for the empire, the nation, and its diaspora. As a number of film scholars have shown, films are ideal media for the mixing of thoughts and perceptions, objects and subjects, the sensory and the verbal, the narrative and the pictorial, and the aural and the visual. While films are crucial in bringing different cultures into the same frame of reference and connecting them with each other for the purpose of consumerism, they also have the capacity to cross the threshold of colonial modernity and its boundaries as in the case of the outreach video. In this context, the carpet is the reiteration of otherness as nation, a mobile commodity itself that enters the transnational marketplace.[52]

One of the important characteristics of transnational commodities is that they intend to keep "the national culture national even as it becomes global."[53] In this context, the carpet stands for the reiteration of otherness as nation, a mobile commodity itself that enters the transnational marketplace. Thus, Oriental carpets, like ships, trains, and airplanes, become sites of time travel between the past and the present, the religious and the secular, the private and the public, the primitive and the civilized, the image and the material object, and the real and the virtual imagining of a highly mobile object that can fly anywhere. The carpet seems to be like a ship, in motion in modernity, a metaphor and a sign for mobility and imagination, "a heterotopia of illusion or compensation."[54]

Between Fantasy and Flight

In this chapter, I have shown how and why Oriental carpets became a civilizational commodity and a component of the spectacular Orient that could be bought and sold through an economy of affects. This affective economy emerged from the convergence of a few ideas. First of all, carpets as auratic objects animated cultural difference, abstracting the sensuous desire for tactility. Second, carpets as mnemonic objects remained a site of cultural continuity, merging the technologies of memory with the technologies of self in everyday life. Third, carpets as boundary objects belonging to the realm of magic in Orientalist discourse inspired the scientific and popular imagination. Finally, Oriental carpets' design, both spatially and aesthetically, was used to distinguish the Orient and the Occident, ensuring their material and aesthetic reproduction. The affective economy that regulated the consumption of Orientalia made the

Persian carpet into an exotic thing from a faraway culture; the more value was invested in its difference, the more it became seductive and desirable.

The flying carpet indexed otherness within the bourgeois subject of colonial modernity, connecting European imagination with the history of colonialism and modern hierarchies of race, class, gender, and culture. These material objects, fetishized visually and discursively as establishing the proper boundaries between persons/things, us/them, primitive/modern, Oriental/Occidental, and female/male, covered over anxieties about race, class, and gender.

The popularity of such fantasy objects is linked with the development of masculinist sciences and technologies influenced by militarist and imperialist impulses in colonial modernity, as well as the feminization of labor and its concealment in a capitalist economy. As I showed in this chapter, the Oriental flying carpets have inspired the aerial imagination of the Western military industry as an airborne carrier. Paradoxically, the carpet industry still heavily relies on pre-modern weaving technologies while the flying carpets of the West, superior in their technological sophistication and their capacities for aerial surveillance and destruction, are sent back to maintain a new form of empire.[55] As Warner points out, "The worlds of science and fantasy do not invariably clash—one can nourish the other."[56]

An interrogation of the operation of the empire through territorial and political claims to power has been central to a critical postcolonial perspective; however, the story of informal imperialism as well as the complicity of the empire in entertainment, consumerism, and the military-industrial complex still needs to be told. The networks of peaceful means of free trade, consumerism, and economic integration, as well as modes of knowledge production in the age of global media and new information technologies, have been crucial in the establishment of the old and new forms of empire.

Notes

1. Published in Lawrence Winters, *Rugs and Carpets From the Orient* (New York: Claflin, 1902[?]). Owning a prayer carpet as a commodity means taming, domesticating, and emptying its religious and sacred function. According to some museum commentators, "Few Mohammedans of Persia will sell prayer rugs to infidels, but in other Mohammedan countries such rugs are manufactured expressly for the Western Trade" ("Maksoud of Kashan and Mrs. McCormik of Chicago. Great carpets and great collectors: the painted, well-nigh priceless wool of Persia," in *Fortune* 2, no. 4 (October 1930): 53, author not mentioned).

2. For an analysis of the prayer carpets, see Minoo Moallem, "Praying Through the Senses: The Prayer Rug/Carpet and the Converging Territories of the Material and the Spiritual," *MAVCOR Journal,* Center for the Study of Material and Visual

Cultures of Religion (New Haven, CT: Yale University, 2014). https//mavcor.yale.edu/conversations/essays/praying-through-senses.

3. Oriental things included what was referred to as Chinoisrie, Indiennerie, Turquerie, etc.

4. Thomas Kim, "Being Modern: The Circulation of Oriental Objects," *American Quarterly* 58, no. 2 (June 2006): 388.

5. Ibid.

6. Samuel Weber, *Targets of Opportunity: On the Militarization of Thinking* (New York: Fordham University Press, 2005), 101.

7. Gregory J. Seigworth and Melissa Gregg, eds., *The Affect Theory Reader* (Durham, NC: Duke University Press, 2010), 1.

8. Jacques Rancière, *The Politics of Aesthetics: The Distribution of the Sensible* (London and New York: Continuum, 2004). Affects have been defined as moments of intensity, as the connection between the somatic and the social, the body and the world, or even vitalism and affective responses to things. See Gilles Deleuze and Felix Guattari, *What Is Philosophy?* (New York: Columbia University Press, 1994); Brian Massumi, *Politics of Affect* (Cambridge: Polity Press, 2015); Eve Kosofsky, *Touching Feeling: Affect, Pedagogy, Performativity* (Durham, NC: Duke University Press, 2003).

9. Weber, *Targets of Opportunity*, 26.

10. Rey Chow, "Fateful Attachments: On Collecting, Fidelity, and Lao She," *Critical Inquiry* 28, no. 1, Things (Autumn 2001): 286–304.

11. Karl Marx refers to two concepts—productive consumption and consumptive production—to point out that "production is consumption and consumption is production." *Grundrisse, Foundations of the Critique of Political Economy* (London: Penguin Group, 1973[1939]). He argues that consumption creates the need for new production. In his view, "Production creates the material, as external object; consumption creates the need, as internal object, as aim, for production" (*Grundrise*, 253).

12. As I will show in Chapter 4, the nation started to invest in these commodities as an affective attachment to the past.

13. John Plotz, *Portable Property: Victorian Culture on The Move* (Princeton, NJ: Princeton University Press, 2008).

14. Deborah Cohen, *Household Gods: The British and Their Possessions* (New Haven, CT: Yale University Press, 2009), 2.

15. Cited by Ludovic Leonelli, *La Séduction de Baudrillard* (Paris: École Nationale Des Beaux-arts, 2007), 108.

16. Hsu-Ming Teo, *Desert Passions: Orientalism and Romance Novels* (Austin: University of Texas Press, 2012), 121. The desire for Orient as Ali Behdad has argued refers to the political, social, cultural, and psychological factors at work in producing Orientalism in *Belated Travelers: Orientalism in the Age of Colonial Dissolution* (Durham, NC: Duke University Press, 1994), 136.

17. Madeleine Dobie, *Trading Places: Colonization and Slavery in Eighteenth-Century French Culture* (Ithaca, NY: Cornell University Press, 2010), 63.

18. Thorstein Veblen, *The Theory of the Leisure Class* (New York: Dover Publications, 1994[1899]) (1899[1934]), Roland Barthes, *Mythologies* (Paris: éditions du Seuil, 1957) and *L'empire des Signes* (Paris: éditions du Seuil, 2007), and Pierre Bourdieu, *La Distinction, Critique Sociale du Jugement* (Paris: Editions de Minuit, 1979).*La Distinction.*

19. Georg Simmel, "Money and Commodity Culture," in *Simmel on Culture*, eds. David Frisby and Mike Featherstone (Thousand Oaks, CA: Sage Publications, 1997), 244.

20. Georg Simmel, "Fashion, Adornment and Style," in *Simmel on Culture*, eds. David Frisby and Mike Featherstone, (Thousand Oaks, CA: Sage Publications, 1997), 215–216.

21. Weber, *Targets of Opportunity*, 102.

22. For a comprehensive analysis of the intertwined histories of empire and vision in modernity see Martin Jay and Ramaswamy (eds) *Empires of Vision* (Durham and London: Duke University Press, 2014).

23. Jeffrey A. Auerbach, *The Great Exhibition of 1851: A Nation on Display* (New Haven, CT: Yale University Press, 1999), 102.

24. For some examples of what was exhibited in these exhibitions, see www.tehranprojects.com/Early-Iranian-Pavilions-at-the-World-Expos.

25. As noted by James Clifford, museums are contact zones, sites of identity-making and transculturation. James Clifford, Routes. *Travel and translation in The Late Twentieth Century* (Cambridge: Harvard University Press, 1997), 219.

26. Wilhelm R. Valentiner, Curator of Decorative Arts, A Catalogue of a Loan Exhibition of Early Oriental Rugs, The Metropolitan Museum of Art, New York, November 1, 1910–January 15, 1911, xviii.

27. *Engineering Weekly,* July 4, 1873, Vol. XVI, 1.

28. Alison Blunt and Robyn Dowling, *Home* (New York and London: Routledge, 2006), 145.

29. Madeleine Dobie, *Trading Places*, 95.

30. *Times,* January 9, 1919, p. 3, issue 41993; col. F.

31. Caren Kaplan, author's statement, "Dead Reckoning: Aerial Perception and the Social Construction of Targets," From author's statement, *Vectors Journal* 2, no. 2 (Winter 2007).

32. *Times,* May 27, 1920; p. 15; issue 42421; col. F.

33. Marina Warner, *Stranger Magic: Charmed States and the Arabian Nights* (Cambridge, MA: Harvard University Press, 2011), 67.

34. Ron Machado, an aviator, author, and instructor, cited in *Flying Carpet: The Soul of an Airplane* (Aviation Supplies & Academics, Inc., 2007), iii.

35. Cited in https://nazmiyalantiquerugs.com/blog/artist-explores-flying-rugs-childhood/. David Schorr is an artist and professor of art. In his series of paintings called *Flying Carpet*, exhibited in New York City in 2016, he revisits his childhood memory of playing on his grandmother's Persian rugs.

36. Warner, *Stranger Magic*, 331.

37. Kajri Jain, *Gods in the Bazaar: The Economics of Indian Calendar Art* (Durham, NC: Duke University Press, 2007), 18.

38. For example, as noted by Federhen et al: In nineteenth-century America, the self-conscious sensuality was translated into textile rich interiors. Layers of Oriental carpets, cushions, hassocks, ottomans and voluptuously over-upholstered seating forms provided a form of pleasure that was morally acceptable to middle-class Americans in contrast to the perceived sexual licentiousness of Middle Eastern cultures. Deborah Anne Federhen, Bradley C. Brooks and Lynn A. Brocklebank, Accumulation & Display. Mass Marketing Household Goods in America, 1880–1920 (Delaware: The Henry Francis du Pont Winterthur Museum, 1986) 64.

39. The first collection and translation was in French by Orientalist and archeologist Antoine Galland, entitled *Les Mille et Une Nuit*. It was then translated into English by British geographer and Orientalist Sir Richard Francis Burton a century later.

40. *Arabian Nights*, 1991, 139.

41. Warner, *Stranger Magic*, 67.

42. The fetish of the flying carpet, as a domesticated and desired commodity, may have something to do with the history of the persecution of broomstick witches in Europe that gave rise to masculinist and militarist science and technology, making permanent the effects of slavery and exploited feminized labor. Commodities may be turning the traumatic memory of witch-burning, slavery, and displacement of masses of people in modernity into repeatable commodities.

43. See www.themagiccarpet.biz/oriental-rugs-d2/.

44. Asterix was originally a French comic character invented in the late 1950s. Asterix lives in a village in the Roman Empire and is a modern adventurer who travels to many countries, including Persia and Egypt. The Asterix character has generated many commodities, including toys, cartoons, and amusement parks.

45. Since its development in the early twentieth century, the animation industry has grown to be a vast profit-making sector of US and world cinema.

46. http://disney.wikia.com/wiki/Magic_Carpet.

47. As demonstrated by feminist film scholar Gina Marchetti, with the rise of corporate capitalism, films and the motion picture as part of a broader interest in the Orient disseminated a new ideology of consumption, turning the domestic sphere into a site of leisure, comfort, and consumerism. See Gina Marchetti, *Romance and the "Yellow Peril": Race, Sex, and Discursive Strategies in Hollywood Fiction* (Berkeley: University of California Press, 1993), 26–28.

48. Several movies with similar (if not the same) plots were made later on, including *Le Voleur de Bagdad*, 1946 (French version of the original *The Thief of Bagdad*); *Baghdad Thirudan* in Tamil by T. P. Sundaram in 1960; and *Il Lardo de Bagdad* in Italy in 1961.

49. As noted by Ella Shohat, "Generally these films superimposed the visual traces of civilizations as diverse as Arab, Persian, Chinese and Indian into a single portrayal of the exotic Orient, treating cultural plurality as if it were a monolith." Gedner in Hollywood's Orient (*Middle East Report* 162 (January–February, 1990)). Also, see

Ella Shohat, ed., *Talking Visions: Multicultural Feminism in a Transnational Age* (Cambridge, MA: MIT Press, 2001).

50. There are many songs and music performances that use the trope of the flying carpet. The award-winning "Magic Carpet Ride," a song written by John Kay and Rushton Moreve based on an album that was released in 1968, is a great example. The ride on the magic carpet promises a fantasy world that will set the girls free. The sound, like the flying carpet, is supposed to take one away. Here the promise of the heterosexual romance is to set the female character free. "A Whole New World," an award-winning song made for Disney's *Aladdin*, is another example. The song turns the "shinning, shimmering, splendid carpet as a vehicle to 'a whole new world.'" Again, through the song and the sound of the music, Aladdin promises to take Jasmine not only to a fantasy world but to a "fantastic point of view" where "no one to tell us no or where to go."

51. See http://payvand.org/#payvand.

52. As noted by Abdul JanMohamed, "this kind of fetishization transmutes all the specificity and difference into a magical essence." Abdul R. JanMohamaed, "The Economy of Manichean Allegory: The Function of Racial Difference in Colonialist Literature," in *"Race," Writing, and Difference*, ed. Henri Louis Gates, Jr. (Chicago: University of Chicago Press, 1986), 86.

53. Plotz, *Portable Property*, 22.

54. Foucault, *Aesthetics, Method, and Epistemology: Essential Works of Foucault, 1954–1984, Vol. 2*, series editor, Paula Rabinow (New York: The New Press, 1998), 185.

55. Down below, in Iraq or Afghanistan, bodies can be bombarded, destroyed, and annihilated; up above is the visual and the virtual, the world of representations.

56. Warner, *Stranger Magic*, 342.

3

THE SPECTACLE OF LABOR

Figure 3.1 **The camera targets the weavers and frames them on the screen. The place gets to
be subordinated to the time, to the eternal time of what is captured in the screen, a
time closed up to the possibility of pain, death, hardship, love, passion, and pleasure. Once circulated as an image, it becomes legible through its referentiality to
other images.**

Photographed by Antoin Sevruguin

As I argued in the last two chapters, in the mid-nineteenth century, Oriental
carpets became an attractive commodity and, shortly after, shifted from a luxury item to a mass-produced product. The mass production of Oriental carpets
in general and Persian carpets in particular concurred with the emergence of

middle classes in the West. This transformation coincided with the aesthetic distinction of racial, gender, and class differences that made it possible for the affordable production of carpets. While the antique carpets were either muse-umized or continued to be kept in antique shops or bourgeois houses, access to the skilled but cheap labor force in the colonial and semi-colonial countries enabled massive importation of the hand-knotted carpets to Europe and the United States. The Orientalization of the carpets and their circulation coin-cided with the transnationalization of exploitative labor. Some scholars refer to this process as the international division of labor, but I prefer to refer to it as the transnationalization of exploitative labor, arguing that it would be difficult to separate labor, capital, and systems of representations from each other beyond the sphere of economy. Most literature on the internationalization of labor dis-misses questions of representations, including the significance of the affective economy and consumptive production of the Oriental carpets.

In this chapter, I argue that while the spectacle of the commodity was crucial in commodity fetishism and concealment of the labor, we also need to interro-gate what I call "the spectacle of labor." What I mean by this is a particular display of labor that complements the discursive construction of the Oriental Other as primitive, unskilled, and predisposed to intensive manual work.[1] Indeed, as many scholars argue, the British Empire not only managed to finance the industrial revolution through colonial occupation and theft of resources but also through transnational trade and transfer of the most exploitative segments of the market. In this context, gendered Orientalism as a discourse, as a knowl-edge frame, and as the rationalization of a transnational gendered division of labor became an integral part of the mass production of Orientalia, including Persian carpets.

The space of what was called the harem became a natural site of Orien-tal women's work, while the bourgeois home was redeemed as a site of con-sumption. The construction of an Eastern masculinity and femininity in the gendered Orientalist discourse served many purposes. Most importantly this gendered discourse provided a rational for the transfer of the most exploit-ative parts of labor to semi-colonized or colonized countries. Gender was a central component of cultural difference beyond ethnic, class, and urban/rural/tribal differences. As I demonstrated in the last chapter, the Oriental-ist discourse constructed Muslim men as indulging in the pleasure of taking advantage of the women of their harems and Muslim women as inclined to live a submissive life. Gradually, this discourse and imagery naturalized the exploitation of women and children's labor force as a component of Eastern despotism and patriarchy. Persian women's exploitation in the carpet industry was not only justified by their cultural and religious backwardness but also naturalized as beneficial for the consumptive production of British and US imperialism.[2]

The visual depiction of carpet weavers in Iran went hand in hand with the carpet connoisseurs' discourse and represented carpet weavers as rural, tribal women, as Chapter 1 indicated. This trend continues to the present, expanding to carpet-selling websites. The discourse and imaginary of civilizational commodities not only created space to disconnect from labor via commodity fetishism à la Marx, but also showed labor in a way that was consistent with "the aesthetic of disappearance of the damaged human body," in Rey Chow's terms.[3] Also, the spectacularization of labor as rural and tribal perpetuated colonial ideas of Oriental labor as feminized and tribal by empowering a masculinist patriarchal system. Furthermore, the spectacle of labor concealed the industrialization of the carpet industry along with the expansion of small- and medium-sized family-owned workshops by constructing them as primitive and unchanging. As Guy Debord notes, "The spectacle is not a collection of images; rather it is a social relationship between people that is mediated by images."[4] This social relationship enabled the cohabitation of capitalism and patriarchy in trade and the regulation of labor while establishing a racialized division of labor.[5]

The consumptive production of Persian carpets created two interconnected realms: labor and leisure. Both of these realms were feminized[6] since one was depicted as a site of middle-class and upper-middle-class consumerism aligning carpets with women—not only as consumers of the carpets but sometimes as carpets themselves by converging women with the carpet—and the other as a site of rural and tribal women's labor. Both of these realms constructed carpet weaving as an extension of the natural desires and capacities of Persian women's bodies. Whereas the male elite in England, the United States, and other parts of Europe controlled the ownership of the carpets along with their trade and circulation, Iranian men became implicated either in mediating the labor in the households and in small- and medium-sized workshops or as carpet factory workers.

From Kidderminster to Sultanabad

To illustrate the spectacle of labor and the representation of leisure, I start with the history of the carpet industry and transnational labor exploitation in Kidderminster, England. Kidderminster is in the district of Worcestershire, Southeast of Birmingham, England. It became the center of British carpet industry in the eighteenth and nineteenth centuries. In the course of my research at the Kidderminster carpet archives, I not only studied the carpet archives but also interacted with some people involved in the carpet industry. During my stay there, I was able to visit one of the very last carpet factories, which was producing modern wall-to-wall carpets, mostly for hotels in the United States. As opposed to the image projected onto the Oriental carpet industry, the plant was organized based on a gendered division of labor, most factory workers were white working-class men who mostly worked on weaving and dyeing, while women worked on repairing mistakes.[7] One of the archivist, who used to work in the company as an engineer, reminded me that the factory was one of the very last carpet-producing sites in the town given that since 1965, Kidderminster had been less and less involved in carpet production.

Kidderminster was the center of the cloth-weaving industry. However, in the nineteenth and early twentieth centuries, the city gradually transformed into producing more industrialized, modern carpets. In July 1826, on the occasion of the visit of the Duke of York, Kidderminster's workers showed him their imitation of the famous Ardebil carpet (a dazzling handmade carpet from the Iranian Safavid era) that they made using power looms. At that time, given the growing demand for the Oriental carpets, Kidderminster factories started to make copies in England. Impressed by the stunning Ardebil carpet, in his Town Hall speech, the Duke observed:

> After what you have shown me, I am at a loss to understand why the public are inclined to prefer modern Oriental carpets when they can obtain such beautiful ones made by British labor: and I assure you that I shall do everything in my power to draw attention to your magnificent production.[8]

Becoming a center of the carpet industry, new technologies of weaving including the power looms as well as Chenille looms were implemented. If we take the moment of Kidderminster's workers attempt to reproduce the Ardebil carpet as a turning point in the British carpet industry to replace hand-knotted Persian carpets with the mass-produced machine-made carpets, we should conclude that this did not last for a long time. Carpet weavers in many locations in Europe revolted, interrupting the exploitative conditions of the carpet industry.[9] These strikes put an end to the Duke of York's encouragement of British Labor to continue its hand-knotted carpet production via more technologically advanced carpet looms. In its place, there opened up a new chapter in the transnationalization of the carpet-weaving industry, and the transfer of the most exploitative parts of labor to England's colonized or semi-colonized peripheries. India and Persia began to be represented as "the great carpet nations" under the direct or indirect rule of "the rising sun of the British Empire with its meridian power and splendor warm."[10]

Historically, the trade between Europe and Iran was limited until the early nineteenth century, however by the beginning of the twentieth century, British Empire expanded its networks in Iran through the East India Company as well as many other British companies that established themselves in the south and central parts of Iran and elsewhere. This new expansion of the British Empire to Iran had a significant impact on the commodification of carpets while it pushed other commodities out of the commodity circle. For example, both silk and cotton, which used to be produced in Iran, were de-commoditized because of the massive import of British goods to Iran via India. As a result, hand-knotted Persian carpets, even before the exploration and colonization of oil, became major products due to their quality and popularity in Europe and access to the cheap labor force in Iran.

According to Denis Wright, the British Empire made the renewal of diplomatic relations conditional upon the signature of a commercial treaty protecting the interest of British trade in Iran.[11] Some companies settled in Tabriz, Arak, Isfahan, and Kashan and started to produce handmade carpets in various parts of Iran. These businesses included Ziegler and Co.; The Persian Carpet Manufacturing Co, a subsidiary of Hotz; and The Oriental Carpet Manufacturers Ltd, (O.C.M.). Also, some smaller British firms, including Gray, Paul and Co.; Lynch Bros Trading; and The Persian Gulf Trading Co., established carpet manufacturing in various parts of Iran, especially Tabriz, Sultanabad (currently Arak), and Isfahan.[12]

The map shown here (figure 3.2), from the 1920s, highlights the location of oil and carpets as major commodities, collapsing Iran's territories with its commodity production.

Ziegler & Co. (British-Swiss company) was one of the first and largest Western companies involved in the carpet trade in Iran and operated from Birmingham, England. In 1860, Ziegler established itself in Tabriz, a major commercial center in the north of Iran at that time, mostly trading silk and cotton. According to Carol Bier,

In spite of the complaints of Iranian merchants and their resistance, European imports reached a peak in Iran in the middle of the nineteenth century. But the decline of textile manufacturing in Iran was difficult to reverse. The most effective effort, however, was that attempted by foreign capitalists who sought to commercialize rug weaving to suit the new demands of the European market. Towards the end of the nineteenth century, investment and capitalization of local and foreign firms in Iran instigated development of the Persian carpet industry. Income from the sale of carpets supplanted that once derived from the export of silk.[13]

Figure 3.2 **Colonial Map of Iran**

After settling its carpet manufacturing factories in Sultanabad (Arak) in 1891, Ziegler had a major role in the domestication of the carpets and their consumption for the European households, including adopting the carpets to the scale of the room and its furnishing as well as their manufacturing in terms of color and design.[14] By 1894, the company had operations in more than 111 villages in the Sultanabad area; they bought land and created a compound there, and hired some designers to create sketches of carpet weaving.[15]

Figure 3.3 **Carpet Sketches by British Designers and Travelers from the Late Nineteenth and Early Twentieth Century**
Photographed by Minoo Moallem

Competition between the British and the Russians prevented the complete settlement of the British in Iran. Also, many Iranian entrepreneurs started to compete with the British in controlling the carpet industry. This competition, as well as resistance to the colonial control of the Iranian products, had three consequences. One was the upsurge of local carpet merchants, the second was the reinforcement of local patriarchies and home-based carpet production closed to the penetration of the European firms, and the third was the increasing collaboration of the Iranian traders and entrepreneurs, especially those concentrated in the local bazaars in various cities. With the de-commodification of silk and cotton, Persian carpets became one of the country's major export items in the early twentieth century.[16] With the establishment of the modern nation-state, both carpets and oil became the first and the second most valuable commodities, paving the way for the formation of a national male elite to collaborate, negotiate, and eventually compete to regain control over imperial domination.

The transfer of labor to the so-called East, or Orient, resolved the labor crisis in Europe and transformed Persian carpets from luxury objects into a mass-consumed commodity. Though most industrialized factory-made carpets were produced in Europe, the most labor-consuming, handmade tasks were exported to the colonized or semi-colonized worlds. Hence, the establishment of a new division of labor not only relied on gender, class, and race but also on geopolitical location. It was within this transnational and colonial division of labor that the notions of home and market, leisure and labor, object and subject, and the Orient and the Occident gained purchase to help save the British carpet industry.

Many carpet connoisseurs were involved in the establishment of British carpet factories in Iran. Cecil Edwards, who has written a classic book on Persian carpets, was one of the main Persian rug connoisseurs.[17] Edwards was the son of an English businessman who took over his father's import-export family business in Constantinople in 1907 to form a new transnational company, the Oriental Carpet Manufacturers, or OCM, with its headquarters in Smyrna. His letters from Tehran to the family of his wife, Clara, in the United States tell not only a lot about the involvement of the British in the Iranian carpet industry but also about the competition of various trading companies to control the Persian carpet industry in Iran.[18]

The establishment of the carpet empire, as well as other European firms under British protection, changed the nature of carpet production in Iran in significant ways. First of all, production became subordinated to the consumption of carpets by Western countries, changing the direction of productive consumption to consumptive production. Second, the limited production of carpets, either as luxury objects or village craft, was transformed into a mass-produced commodity. Third, given the unfamiliarity of the British with Iranian society, the need for mediation created a group of Iranian dealers and entrepreneurs who arbitrated between foreign companies and local labor. Fourth, carpet design started to be tailored to European taste. And finally, the dyeing process changed radically with the importation of chemical dyes to Iran.[19] The replacement of vegetal dyes with low-quality, cheaper, and toxic chemical dyes facilitated the mass production of handwoven carpets, creating space for European firms to take control of the carpet industry. The introduction of chemical dyes meant the decline of this mostly local, male-dominated part of the carpet industry and the beginning of the reorganization of labor, which included both the composition of labor as well as its regulation.

Toxic Convenience

Dyeing practices accompanied the mass production of Persian carpets due to the importation of animal coloring and coal tar products by the British to Iran. Nicolas Fokker notes that the artificial or synthetic dyes were developed in the mid-nineteenth century from a waste product of coal tar. He makes the point that in the carpet industry there is a distinction between natural and artificial dyes. Natural dyes refer to the organic dyes extracted from indigo, saffron, madder root, henna, bark, fruit peel, different plant leaves, etc. They may also be obtained from animal substances, including cochineal, for the red color.[20] The desire for duller colors, in response to European and American tastes, along with the need for further division of labor and faster production changed local dyeing practices. This took place rapidly, since synthetic dyes made Western countries independent of expensive tropical plants while Iranian labor became more dependent on the European import.[21]

The Iranian government did indeed resist this process at the time. According to George Griffin Lewis, "In 1903 a law was enacted by the Persian Government forbidding the importation of chemical dyes and seizing and destroying all fabrics in which they are used."[22] The impact of the aniline dyes was devastating for the workers, given the damage it caused to pulmonary as well as reproductive functions, to mention just a couple of side effects. Of course, the bad quality of the carpets and the damaging effects of chemical dye on the reputation of the Persian carpets in the eyes of Western consumers motivated the Iranian government's resistance, though this resistance did not necessarily stem from a concern about labor conditions or the damaging effects of chemical dyes on the weavers' health.

The Western consumers' demands for specific colors and the increasing takeover of the carpet industry by British and other Western companies also facilitated this process, and soon aniline colors were used all over, especially taking over the wool industry. According to John Kimberly Mumford, "Originality in design was discontinued, forbidden, and chemical dyes were introduced."[23] He also notes, "Even when the dyes are vegetable products they are mordanted by chemical methods and the old formula for preparing and fixing them seem to have been lost."[24] As a result, according to Gans-Ruedin, between 1913 and 1914, 58 percent of exported Iranian carpets used chemical dyes.[25] Emmett Eiland, a rug connoisseur, claims,

> By shortly after World War II, for all practical purposes, natural dyes in Oriental rugs were a thing of the past. The only way one could own a rug with natural dyes was to inherit it or buy an old one. Of course, as the quality of new carpets declined, the cost of old rugs began to rise.[26]

Chemical dyes slowly replaced natural dyes. Currently, carpets are mostly produced with chemical dyes, but a small part of the industry still makes carpets using natural colors. The expansion of the manufacturing of chemical dyes and cheap synthetic materials did not raise any concern around workers' health. The new division of labor between the chemical dye manufacturers and the spinning factories, along with yarn and wool imports, pressured the weavers to purchase these commodities from middlemen. The brokers acquired these goods from the manufacturers while selling them to the weavers. This process made the weavers more dependent on the dyed yarn provided by the middlemen. This procedure reduced the need for local workers who were involved in the production of natural dyes. As a result of both the large-scale production of Persian carpets and the new division of labor, Iranian labor became dependent on the chemical dyes imported from the West as well as the expertise to use it properly in the carpet industry. Furthermore, due to lower cost of dying, increasingly the carpets made with the low quality, toxic aniline became popular.

Currently, according to Amin, the owner of a major carpet company in Iran, only 2 percent of carpets are being made with natural colors. Most of these carpets are special orders. He also noted that the wool these days is mostly imported from Australia and Korea, because it is costly to produce wool in Iran.

Domesticating the Carpet

In the early twentieth century, a transnational division of labor was at the center of the imperial nexus of power. The colonized world was depicted in its capacity to produce goods. In the example of Iran, both oil and carpets were mapped out and tracked down as the most valuable commodities. While Iran was not formally colonized, European countries, especially Britain, and eventually the United States controlled both oil and carpets. For example, before the Iranian revolution of 1979, 85 percent of carpets were exported to the United States.

Along with this mapping and with the advent of advertisement, the carpet was domesticated and became a component of middle-class home furniture. One important aspect of the carpet becoming part of the domestic space relates to the transformation of the home at the center of the colonial world in the nineteenth century. Deborah Cohen argues that the British love affair with the domestic interior had a significant influence in domesticity and "house pride."[27] In her view, we inherited the materialist world that the Victorians made.[28] She notes that the notion of morality in Victorian England became lingua franca for evaluating furnishings as a form of spiritual thriving.[29] Also, as argued by Elaine Fleetwood "The ideology of industrial capitalism functions best at a safe remove from its process—in London, or Paris. It can even move to the countryside, to the provinces; it just can't run smoothly in the factory or in the factory town."[30]

While authors such as Amy Kaplan have brilliantly shed light on the connection between the discourse of domesticity, imperial expansion, and nation building, the field is wide open for more scholarship on the material culture of imperial expansion, its aesthetic appeal, and everyday forms of consumption.[31] The juxtaposition of the commodity with the home is reflected in the "Home, Sweet Home" song performed at the opening ceremony of The Colonial and Indian Exhibition, in 1886.[32] The emergence of a popular home culture can be linked to three major transformations; first of all the construction of the home as a site of leisure as opposed to the market as a site of labor; second, the invention of the home as a place of consumption not production; and third, the formation of the home as a haptic space, in Laura Marks' words, meaning an area that "invites not distant contemplation but intimate involvement, the eyes moving over the surface as though touching it."[33]

In this process, commodity spectacle became a site of both unity and difference. As Anne McClintock notes, the cult of domesticity and the new imperialism found a mediatory function in commodities.[34] The capacity of both empire and nation to organize a sense of popular collective unity relied on the management of mass national-commodity spectacle. This process included the construction of the need for Persian carpets as a component of middle-class heteronormative families. It also included the projection of use value and women's work along with the othering of non-Western cultures as belonging to an eternal form of primitiveness, or what McClintock calls the "prehistoric realm."[35] Additionally, this process made space for the formation of the modern Iranian nation's retrieval of an anterior time to reclaim the eternal and primordial essence of the nation through both ethnic and gender difference.

Two recurring images in this context serve to construct not only commodities but also the figure of upper-class and middle-class women as consumers of home culture, as well as invest carpets themselves with a trade value. For example, an early ad from Le Printemps store in Paris (included in the opening of chapter 3) depicts a family (husband, wife, and child) shopping for an Oriental carpet as the salesman describes the carpet. A number of other ads also represent Oriental carpets as a place of domestic comfort for women, men, and children. Like women, children seem to be present in many ads as consumers of domestic comfort and leisure, not as producers or laborers.

Figure 3.4 **Domestic comfort and carpet as a cozy surface**
Westend61/Getty Images

Figure 3.5 **Heteronormative Family as a Unit of Consumption**
Westend61/Getty Images

This trend continues in modern advertisement. The mediation of these images and the discourse on Persian women enable the emergence of modern gendered subjectivities. The housewifization of women complements this process, making home a site of leisure and consumption. These images not only mediate the construction of home in Europe, but they travel through the discourse of modernization and Westernization to Iran. It also mediates the establishment of nation-states and modern citizenship by constructing women as both objects of consumption as well as the inhabitants of an "anachronistic space," in Anne McClintock's terms.[36] While family becomes a unit of consumption and not production, it is with the mediation of modern masculinity that middle-class and lower-class women are brought into the world of civilization and modernization. While middle-class women were given the opportunity to leave their atavistic world of timeless Oriental femininity—depicted in Orientalist discourse vis-à-vis Iran as lazy, indulging in sex and food—they enter the consumer culture as *jens*, referring to both genre and commodity.[37] Constructed both as a gendered subject as well as a commodity, women's *jensiat* became a hybrid mixture of their gender, via their essence or their natural biological traits, and their commodity status, characterized by their objecthood and their position as the object of exchange in the marriage market.[38]

Girls Sold to Slavery: The "Aesthetic Value of Helplessness" and the Burden of Humanism

The story of the carpet is told by many contingencies: nationalists, museum curators, connoisseurs, humanists, and feminists. One of the dominant themes is the story of the pain and suffering of women and children carpet weavers.

Figure 3.6 **The Aesthetic Value of Helplessness**
Photographed by Antoin Sevruguin

This narrative holds together the network that sustains carpet production and consumption. The pain and suffering of carpet weavers generates a sense of guilt. As Walter Benjamin notes in *Capitalism as Religion,* "A situation with no way out produces guilt."[39] Guilt is part of the capitalist mode of production and without it, capitalism cannot regulate itself. Also, regulation based on guilt is necessary for the perpetuation of the super-exploitation of labor.

Indeed, the process of deskilling weavers happened within the context of British factories and continued with the division of labor and paternalistic pro-letarization of urban weavers and workers, along with the patriarchal organiza-tion of labor in the context of households. According to a carpet connoisseur named Benjamin, "They [Messrs Ziegler and Company] keep them [the weav-ers] gradually employed, but one condition is that they shall not give rein to their tastes, but like machines, they shall continually reproduce the designs which are found to meet the prevailing fashion in Europe."[40] This process sepa-rated the weavers from their product and turned them into a carpet-producing machine, while at the same time it kept the idea and the image of the tribal and the rural to exoticize and Orientalize the carpets.

Also, on Monday, April 23rd of 1928, *The Daily Mail* of London in an article entitled "Girls Sold to Slavery" launched a discourse that became a formal part of the rescue industry of humanism for Iranian female carpet weavers. Refer-ring to an article published in the modernist nationalist journal of *Shafaq-e Sorkh* (an early advocate for modernization in Iran and for women's progress),[41] "The cutting off of the offspring of Kerman" criticized the carpet industry's already well-established presence in the Kerman area in which mostly women and girls were working. The *Shafaq-e Sorkh* journal refers to the masses of women and girls who enter "a contract of sale." But the *Daily Mail* translated and interpreted this statement as mothers contracting their six or seven-year-old girls out for four or five years and receiving one-third of the price up front. Shifting the discourse from the contract of sale to blaming mothers for selling their children to the carpet industry fulfilled two purposes. First, it reinforced the discourse on the natural disposition of Persian mothers as bad mothers[42] and, second, it encouraged investment in the bourgeois family and the disciplinary practices of modernization and housewifization. Here the discussion focuses on family hygiene, constructing family as a unified entity regardless of class differences, with motherhood as an extension of women's bodies. This emphasis on motherhood enables the representation of the family as a site of reproduction and consumption rather than production.

The author of *Shafaq-e Sorkh* writes, "These unfortunate creatures are sentenced to death . . . but what a tragic death," and *The Daily Mail* opines, "Even more tragic are the consequences of these lamentable conditions of work on motherhood. Lack of sanitation and continuous work seated on narrow and bare planks affecting deformation and the need for operation in 70 percent of cases."[43] Again, the focus is on motherhood and the impact of work conditions on procreation.

The nationalist journal also attacks "foreign companies that are benefiting from such conditions given that 95 percent of carpet profits go to foreign companies,"[44] setting the stage for the nationalist male elite to take over the carpet industry. The imperial organization of the carpet industry converges with the desire of the local male elite to control the carpet industry relying on family connections and vernacular formal and informal networks facilitated this process. In this case, *The Daily Mail* goes further and establishes a long-lasting humanist discourse on the carpet weavers, enabling a rationale for the reconciliation of the nation and the empire in the years to come.

Labor as a Spectacle

> She weaves as I write
> Creating life is
> What we both care for,
> Tracing time through the thread of our creation
> To the vivacity of here and now!
>
> (My poem)

"Writing does not silence the voice, but awakens it, above all to resurrect so many vanished sisters." Assia Djebar, *Fantasia: An Algerian Cavalcade* (Ortsmouth: Heinemann, 1993), 404.

Figure 3.7 **The Recurring Image of Women at the Loom**
safakcakir/Shutterstock.com

As the previous chapter showed, Persian carpets were displayed and represented as a component of the household, a sign of aristocratic wealth and a
domesticated object that represented the spectacle of the commodity. I argue
that the spectacle of labor complemented the spectacle of the commodity.
Though a significant number of weavers were located in urban areas, the
depiction of weavers in connoisseur books, as well as carpet-selling websites,
is of rural and tribal women. The idea of the rural and the tribal woman as
naturally prone to weaving carpets converges with the market economy to
create a homogenized and permanent basis for the production of the Persian
carpets.

In connoisseur books and online advertisements, the trope of the rural and
tribal woman is produced specifically through repetitious images of rural and
tribal female weavers without any explanation in the text. Women are depicted
either as passive consumers, mostly in voyeuristic roles, rather than as the buyers of the carpet, or as rural and tribal weavers with not much information on
the labor process. For example, George Griffin Lewis in *The Practical Book of
Oriental Rugs* talks about carpet weavers in the following manner:

> A skillful woman weaver will earn from three to six siblings a week and they
> usually work from sunrise to sunset, week after week, month after month,
> year after year. As a rule, they have no education, can neither read nor
> write, and have absolutely nothing else to do but weave and gossip. Rug
> weaving proves a sort of amusement and a source of income; besides they

take a great interest in the work and the height of their ambition is to realize hope of royal recognition for their superior workmanship.[45]

Each book has one or two images that are the same or very similar to each
other in depicting rural or peasant women weaving at the carpet loom. The
weavers of the carpets and any description of the labor process remain the most
concealed and abjectified aspect of the visual representations of the carpets. If
the spectacle of commodity conceals labor, the spectacle of labor excessively
exposes the labor as feminized and tribal, constructing it as unskilled labor.
Cecil Edwards, a well-known Persian carpet connoisseur, denies tribal women
even the ability to think. He writes, "A tribal weaver, as she crouches over her
horizontal loom, is more likely, I think, to seek inspiration from what she sees
than from what she thinks—if, indeed, she thinks at all."[46] Rey Chow's argument
that "our fascination with the native, the oppressed, the savage, and all such
figures is therefore a desire to hold on to an unchanging certainty somewhere
outside our own 'fake' experience"[47]sheds some light on such representations
of the rural and the tribal.

This form of representation continues to the present and uses both the concealment and exposure of commodity and work as fetishes disavowing the colonized and their feminized labor. While carpet-making involves feminine work
on both sides of production and consumption, I refer to this work as "feminized
labor" rather than female labor, given that some workers in the carpet-production
industry, especially in urban areas, are men. However, the feminization of labor
enables an exploitative system that constructs women's work as well as feminized
work as an extension of the workers' body with no or little value. In the past, feminist materialists have argued that the work that is done in the context of home
and within the framework of "the domestic mode of production," in Delphy's
words, is considered non-work or work that is done to reproduce wage labor.[48]
The image that is circulated through carpet advertisements is a "feminized image"
that evacuates the reality of labor conditions for men, women, and children.

As examples, I use a few images that frequently appear in either connoisseur
books or carpet-selling websites to elaborate further on the depiction of rural
and tribal women. These images depict women weavers at the loom. In these
images, the camera mostly approaches women from above or behind. These
recurring images, which are repeated in multiple forms and formats, are part
of what I defined earlier as a scopic economy. This visual economy interpolates
both consuming and producing subjects. The image is supposed to provide a
form of evidence representing a rather coherent narrative of the Persian carpet's production in what McClintock calls "anachronistic spaces," where colonized people, working classes, and women do not inhabit history but exist in

a permanently atavistic time, irrational and bereft of human agency.[49] These images put the viewer in the position of seeing without being seen, referring to the ways in which a display of the labor becomes a spectacle for modern regimes of control and surveillance. It echoes Foucault in making the point that the automatic functioning of power is to arrange things such that "the surveillance is permanent in its effects, even if it is discontinuous in its action."[50] In each image, there is a convergence of surveillance and control in the position of the camera (from above or behind), in the depiction of the tribal and rural female carpet weaver, and in how through the scopic economy power makes itself permanent.

While the specific history of the intersection between capital, labor, and systems of representation in each locality is unique and would require careful genealogical and historical work, representational practices made it possible for distant and historically complex locations to come together without any contradiction, enabling a transnational division of labor as well as the construction of labor and non-labor. The representation of carpet weavers as rural and mostly tribal is part and parcel of this process.[51]

The display of the tribal and rural women is also part of the discourse of development and the exoticization and feminization of poverty. Historically, it gave carpet producing and its condition a unifying face, dismissing the variety of labor forms and labor conditions as well as the artistic and creative process of carpet weaving by making the carpet production into one unified process. The display of the spectacle of labor undermined the possibility and potential for women workers and networks of solidarity and support to organize to improve their situation.

The trope of the carpet weavers' slavery has been perpetuated into the present by an imagery of women and girls at the carpet loom. For example, a contemporary Iranian poet, Houshang Ebtehaj, in one of his well-known poems called "Liberty" writes:

> This carpet lying under your foot,
> Is dyed with blood.
> This flower garlands is made of blood,
> It is the flower of blood. . .[52]

In this recurring image, the female body is overexposed as a site of sexual and cultural difference. Both nation and empire invest in the trope of the female weaver to give meaning to a series of binaries: West/East, us/them, civilized/primitive, male/female, rural/urban, and culture/nature.

In this context, the discussion of labor is detached and disconnected from the transformation of labor, technologies of weaving, and labor conditions—including the increasing industrialization of carpet weaving, the historical rise

Figure 3.8 **Labor as a Spectacle**
© Martin Hürlimann

of urban workshops and factories, and the transnational division of labor. Furthermore, concerns over the humanity of weavers and how weaving leaves them disabled due to dark rooms and long hours of sitting at the loom—as described by some connoisseurs, missionaries, and, more recently, feminists—have been detached and disconnected from the transformation of the carpet industry and its political economy. Furthermore, the depiction of the institution of the family from a unit of production to a unit of consumption in the process of modernization supplemented the separation of exchange value from the value and non-value. In other words, middle-class women started to be targeted as consumers of commodities. And the domestic work of cooking, cleaning, and bearing and rearing of children was concealed as "non-value" for both middle-class and working-class women.

Dehumanizing female labor infused with worn out imagery and melodramatic words is part and parcel of various writings on carpet weavers from the late nineteenth century to the present. Indeed, the consumer demand had much to do with what Campbell calls "the emergence of a new religious ethic of benevolence in which virtue was associated with the charitable feelings of pity and sympathy."[53] While empathy and compassion might provoke individuals' feelings of sympathy, it makes political action impossible once it becomes the foundation for political activism, since it incessantly reproduces the hierarchy between subjects of empathy and objects of commiseration without challenging how this hierarchy and order has been put to work in the first place.[54]

A good example from early twentieth century literature on carpet weavers is writing by Mary Rebecca Stewart Bird, entitled "The Cry of the Children," published by the Church Missionary Society, in 1916: "The tiny toilers in the Eastern lands have need of one, as brave and true as she, to voice their wrongs and make their crying heard in every Christian home. Come with me and watch these carpet-weavers in a Persian town."[55] This statement was the beginning of a sensationalist discourse and launched a bigger focus of attention on women and children carpet weavers in Iran. This early form of humanism developed along with the expansion of the carpet industry, the introduction of chemical dyes, the massive practice of subcontracting, and weaving in the context of the family in rural, tribal, and poor urban areas of Iran.

In this context, the carpet became a signifier and a material object connecting civilization to the world of nature, the primitive, and the female that is fixed in time and space, never able to catch up. A world of primitive looms, dark rooms, and abject bodies provoked the desire for consumption even more. The wounded and suffering body of the weavers becomes a site of affective consumerism. The circulation and representation of such images of the "feminine labor" is part of the value-producing market exchange. The repetitious reference to women's work as the state of nature, as an extension of their bodies, and as non-labor by displacing it on women's suffering becomes a source of symbolic value.

Indeed, the mobilization of affects and emotions serves a "do-good consumerism" more than challenging the social inequality and exploitative conditions women weavers experience. They also create space for a rescue narrative that continues to be used to empower Western imperialist and missionary feminism of both religious and secular backgrounds, justifying old and new forms of colonialism. Also, while feminist literature on women, globalization, and the international and sexual division of labor have contributed enormously to an understanding of the exploitative conditions within which women in the Global South are located, this literature has less to do with the ways in which women negotiate or resist their situation and more with systems of exploitation.[56] Furthermore, the construction of the carpet industry as based on the labor of women and children dismisses the involvement of male weavers in urban workshops and factories.

The figure of the rural and tribal female weaver at the loom separates the carpet from the bodies of the weavers (vital, damaged, deformed, and disfigured) on the one hand and the technologies of weaving on the other hand. The knowledge of the bodies in pain makes the carpet an intimate commodity provoking the desire for consumption. Here the carpets function as fetish objects resolving the contradiction between exposing one form of labor while concealing other types of work. The separation of the body from the image both in its disappearance as well as its overexposure becomes a site of ideological invasion. The image then becomes a placeholder for either a certain kind of presence or a total absence. The representation of weavers at the loom makes selling the carpet rely on "the political economy of surveillance."[57] The consumer takes the position of the surveillant gazer while being surveilled. The position of the camera behind both the consumer and the weaver routinize surveillance, capitalizing on the desire to see without being seen.

The inclusion of these images sometimes goes along with such statements as:

> And how intrinsically interesting is the carpet; how unique its long, eventful story; what an ancestry it has! Back to the time of Adam and Eve . . . she is still spinning in the East—goes the history of weaving, which is also the story of the carpet.[58]

These images depict the weavers in proximity with the natural, the tribal, and the uncivilized, making productivity a necessary condition. They also make the terms of the labor normal, endurable, and tolerable. The image substitutes the body of the weavers, both male and female, through representational intrusion. In broader terms, the Orient is portrayed as tribal and traditional while the Occident is referred to as urban and modern. As a result, civilizations are described as having radically different narratives of origin, which will never come to an end. Being lower on the hierarchy of cultures, the tribal will always be the Other of the urban as well as inferior in the evolutionary stages of civilization in modern narratives of progress and development. In both images, "the primitive," "the tribal," and "the female subject" as "the Other" of civilization wipes out the labor and the process of production. Both the spectacle of commodity and the spectacle of labor use representational practices to dismiss the labor.

The Foucauldian concept of techniques of the self, as methods of psychic organization that function along with the technologies of power and domination to produce docile bodies, is relevant to the spectacle of the tribal and the rural. However, Foucault did not analyze how marketing transforms techniques of the self into modern psycho-technologies of trans-individuation threaded by networks. The question of advertisement or representation, and how this process of trans-individuation and Orientalism form and transform subjectivity, seem to be crucial in the case of Persian carpets as commodities, their representations in relation to the regulation of labor.

The figure of the rural and tribal women at the loom is still massively aestheticized and circulated in carpet-selling websites. The tribal and rural woman is depicted as a target of the consumerist gaze. She is the amalgamation of pre-capitalist patriarchal structures. She is there to provoke a desire for modern consumption of the carpet, for its reproduction, for a symbolic order that makes the tribal and the communitarian the business of the past constructing exploited labor and child labor as pre-modern violence. The rural and tribal woman is turned into a spectacle with an aesthetic value for exchange/a symbolic exchange value. The desire for the consumption of what signifies 'tradition' and in this case the carpet made by tribal and rural women reinvest in an aesthetic dichotomy or even opposition between modern and traditional upholding one of the major myths of colonial modernity. Consuming tradition as belonging to the past conceals the integration of pre-capitalist and patriarchal modes of production within modern forms of industrialized capitalism. The aesthetic value of this spectacle that continues to the present day increases with the weavers' victimization and powerlessness.

In the Gaps

The Persian carpet does not stand for either absence or silence. The carpet's gaps, imperfections, and unevenness can indeed represent both women weavers' experience as well as their authorship. The linkage between the text and the textile constitute this relationship. To move away from the texts and the imagery constructing the women weavers either as victims or as the signifier of the primitive Orientals, I would like to turn to the village of Talie Abad.

Zahra is a carpet weaver in Talie Abad. Carpets are produced in many households in the village. Most men in the community are involved in herding (and occasionally drug trafficking), while women do carpet weaving as well as other tasks related to agriculture and herding. Zahra rents a few carpet looms and hires other women to weave rugs. The women come and go based on their own time. They are paid based on how many rows they have completed and not on an hourly basis. This gives them the flexibility to work on the carpet whenever they can. There is a complex network of collaboration between the women of the village to get all these tasks done promptly and properly. I spent a few hours with six weavers who worked on two carpet looms at Zahra's place; they brought their babies and their old mothers along and took care of them collectively, taking turns or asking their older daughters to take care of the younger ones. They often cook their daily meal before leaving the house or while weaving the carpet. Once in a while, all the weavers would take a break and talk about their families, the new TV series, or their conflicts and problems. The only part of their work that extracts monetary value is their weaving.

Some women in the village work at their homes and have a contract with middlemen. Sakineh, one of my informants, is among them. She has set up her carpet loom in her living room. Her daughter, who goes to primary school, helps her occasionally. She is a good student and Sakineh proudly talks about her good grades. However, Sakineh believes that her daughter should learn carpet weaving, since it will give her skills to make money, and to make friends, no matter where she goes. Sakineh has a son who is two years older and goes to school, but he does not "sit at the loom," as she puts it. Boys are not supposed to weave carpets.

Women weave the carpet along with other tasks as part of their domestic labor, by which I refer to any labor that they do while they weave that is not valued—not because it does not have value, but because it is not considered a value-producing kind of work. Colette Guillaumin, a feminist materialist, calls tasks with "*le charge mental et emotive*" or work with a mental and emotional charge, including taking care of children, the elderly, or the sick, to require deep affect and emotions. She argues that women's time, labor, and energy are appropriated by men, both individually and collectively, and justified by their natural differences.[59]

Zahra, another weaver, is resentful of how people consider the weavers to be non-skilled workers. She notes, "We are highly skilled workers." The only part of the weaving that is done by less-skilled workers, mostly (female) children, is filling in the flowers. The work of weaving these days is not only about a romantic notion of storytelling but part of an informal network of labor working in coordination with the formal system. Indeed, it would be hard to talk about formal and informal sites of production as entirely distinct from each other, as these networks converge to create use value, non-value, and exchange value. Indeed, none of the households where women weave the carpets own any of those carpets. Instead, increasingly, rural people buy machine-made carpets that mimic the

Figure 3.9 **Producers of Handmade Carpets, Consumers of Machine-Made Imitation**
Photographed by Minoo Moallem

same design as some of the Persian carpets. Interestingly, the machine-made Mashhad carpets, with the dominant color combination of red, are popular in the Talie village, while most carpets woven by women are blue and cream, famously known as Nain carpets.

While the latter are being sold in the bazaar or exported to other countries, the cheap factory-produced carpets (mostly made in China) have become new consumer commodities in the rural areas. The perverse logic of producing the carpets for the market and buying them in the market at the same time marks the disappearance of "use value" as well as "non-value" and their abstraction in this process. Consumptive production is the motor behind both forms of consumerism. Here it is not only commodity fetishism that conceals the labor, but the disconnect between the work, its representation, and its exchange value also masks labor relations. This process not only reconciles the formal and the informal regulation of labor but also turns the rural women and carpet producers into consumer citizens participating in the myth of the household as a site of consumption and not production.

Ultimately, however, the weaver is the one who puts the design into action, and she is indeed the one with the power to make things happen. She is positioned in a place where both the pattern and the product could be interrupted, reinvented, and transgressed. She could create a life closed to the panoptical vision of modernity and the rescue industry of humanism. However, she becomes a source of anxicty as well as desire, an object of surveillance, an incarnation of nature as the Other of the culture, and something beyond time and space, a fictional absence. In turning the weaver into a spectacle, the modern scopic economy achieves two things: it turns the laborer into a spectacle by investing value in the image and mobilizes affects and sympathy through the discourse of humanism towards "the helpless Other."

The branding of commodities with an Oriental identification is radically different from other forms of branding. This kind of branding is made within the context of civilizational imperialism and new and old forms of Orientalism, linking the discursive economy of Orientalism to material production under neoliberal forms of governmentality. The identity attached to commodities that target those who "buy to help" makes the consumers not only feel better but also feel included in the empire, obscuring the blatant violence of consumptive production within an uneven geopolitical context. This sensationalist discourse on helping tribal and rural women weavers accompanied the literature from the early twentieth century until the present, even after the US imposition of economic sanctions and its severe impact on Iranian women weavers.[60]

The women's everyday life experiences of weaving in Talie Abad goes against the sensationalist discourse of humanism. Even within an exploitative condition women have managed to maintain some degree of agency by preserving the

carpet weaving both as savoir-faire that makes them indispensable to the production of carpets, as well as savoir-vivre or the knowledge of how to live a life
of connectivity beyond the remoteness and isolation imposed by both local and
global patriarchy and consumer capitalism. While the spectacle of labor inex-
orably reduces women weavers to atavistic beings imprisoned in an antiquated
temporality, they are the creators of the carpet as one of the oldest and the most
effective result of a weblike system of working, fetishized in the spectacle and
masked as excess beyond it.

The Work of the Spectacle

To conclude, it would be impossible to understand questions of exploitation
without examining the politics of vision, ways of seeing, and practices of mediation and mediatization. While it would be difficult to discuss what constitutes
this form of labor or, better conceptualized, this type of work, this process
keeps both subjects and objects in the same commodity chain. The affective
investment in the image of a helpless Other produces value or a form of a form
of cultured feelings in Lori Merish's terms,[61] in Lori Merish's terms, that serves
humanism as a site of affective action. In this context, it is necessary to interrogate the politics of representation as not limited to the temporality of here and
now but in its historical context. Also, the spectacle of labor complements the
spectacle of commodities in both concealing and revealing the mediatic technologies of oppression and exploitation. This is also challenging humanism
in feminism, one of the most enduring forms of imperialist feminist discourse
always redefining and rationalizing what I call the politics of "sisterhood in
victimization" by separating the human from the machine, the machine from
the techniques, and the labor from the nexus of imperial power.

It is imperative to ask how the desire to consume the image of a passive victim
(as it circulates from the global South to the global North and not vice versa)
also has become complicit in—if not serving—the masculinist and phallogo-
centric desire of a heterosexist order. Here, indeed, the political economy converges with a sexual economy that is investing in both exchange and use value,
suppressing and abjectifying non-value. Without attempting to write the story of
the carpet from the weavers' point of view, given that my focus here is the carpet
as a commodity, one could ask whose experience—both the ability to know and
to know how to live—is absorbed in apparatuses of production, circulation, and
consumption, in commodities, in machines, in expert systems, and in networks.
The answer is that both women's weavers' experiences and their authorship is
suppressed in this process.

The spectacle of labor is facilitated with the discourse of humanism. The discourse of humanism and its interest in social subjects turns indeed into another

way of governing consumptive production. The body of the weavers that is projected into the spectacle of labor is used to sell the carpets. The humanistic concern with the suffering of the women and children as characteristic of Oriental and Muslim societies serve as a symbolic exchange and a "simulated intimacy" between consumers and advertisers in Baudrillard terms.[62] Humanism as a transnational discourse cannot be separated from labor, commodity, production, and consumption. As a discourse, it cannot be understood without a transnational perspective. In this context, humanism glues together the horrified gaze of the British Society at the women and children in Persia that were dying at the carpet loom at the time when England invested massively in the carpet industry in Iran. This gaze continues to purchase value through circulation of the spectacle of labor. It is crucial to understand the linkage between the culture and the economy to find out the subjects' (those who are involved in the production of the carpets) ability to act. The discourse of humanism creates space for those who take action on behalf of the oppressed, yet disengage with the possibility of transgression, negotiation, and resistance by those subjected to exploitation.

Notes

1. As noted by Thomas Richards, "Spectacle and capitalism became indivisible, a world produced, a world distributed, a world consumed, a world still too much with us." *The Commodity Culture of Victorian England: Advertising and Spectacle 1851–1914* (Stanford, CA: Stanford University Press, 1990), 16.
2. The role of carpet connoisseurs was not limited to research and publication on the topic of Persian carpets, but they were also involved in carpet production, trade, and circulation. Many Oriental carpet connoisseurs were either implicated or became involved in the establishment of the carpet industry in Iran.
3. Rey Chow, *Writing Diaspora: Tactics of Intervention in Contemporary Cultural Studies* (Bloomington: Indiana University Press, 1993), 177.
4. Guy Debord, *The Society of Spectacle* (Austin, TX: Rebel Press, 2000 [1994]), 12.
5. As a result, hand-knotted Persian carpets, even before the exploration and colonization of the oil, became major products due to their quality and popularity in Europe and access to the cheap labor force in Iran.
6. I use the concept of feminization to refer to the ways in which mostly women and children as well as men were subjected to the domestic or domesticated regulation of labor. This domestic mode of production, in Christin Dephy's terms, was parallel to the capitalist mode of production and subjected the workers to limitless work hours, low or no wages, and paternalistic control of fathers, husbands, and workshop owners. A number of Marxist feminists refer to this system as a dual system of capitalist patriarchy. See, among others, Maria Mies, *Patriarchy and Accumulation on a World Scale: Women in the International Division of Labour* (London: Zed

Books, 1986); and Sylvia Walby, *Theorizing Patriarchy* (New York: Wiley-Blackwell, 1991).

7. The factory was not letting anyone who was not working there get a tour. I am grateful to one of the former company engineers, who got special permission for me to visit the factory for a few hours.

8. Souvenir brochure of the Royal Visit to Tomkinson and Adam's Works, reprinted from Furnishing Traders, Kidderminster, 1926.

9. The weavers' strikes started in the early nineteenth century. For example, the carpet weavers went on strike 1828; there were also massive riots and a workers' revolt, followed by a strike in 1830, to contest the manufacturers' plan to cut the weavers' wages by 17 percent; and finally, the big strike of 1853 in the city of Kidderminster. See Melvyn Thompson, *Woven in Kidderminster* (Kidderminster: David Voice Associates, 2000).

10. Sydney Humphries, *Oriental Carpets, Runners and Rugs and Some Jacquard Reproductions* (London: Adam and Charles Black, 1910), 385.

11. Wright, *The English Amongst the Persians*, 95.

12. Denis Wright, *The English Amongst the Persians: During the Qajar Period 1787–1921* (Galway, Ireland: MW Books, 1977), 99–100.

13. Carol Bier, *Woven From the Soul, Spun From the Heart: Textile Arts of Safavid and Qajar Iran, 16th–19th Centuries* (Washington, DC: Textile Museum, 1987), 254.

14. See Arto Keshishian, "Ziegler and Their Carpets" in *The Antique Dealer and Collectors' Guide* (London: Patina Press, 1946), 32–35.

15. For more information see Annette Ittig, "Ziegler's Carpet Cartoons," *Hali* 17, no. 82–87 (April/May 1995), 86. Also see Bouda Etemad, "Une Maison Suisse de Commerce en Perse, Ziegler et Cie. (1890–1934), *Revue Suisse d'Histoire* 37, no. 4 (1987): 412–427.

16. See Gad G. Gilbar, "The Opening Up of Qajar Iran: Some Economic and Social Aspects," *Bulletin of the School of Oriental and African Studies* 49, no. 1 (1986); and Ahmad Seyf, "Iranian Textile Handicrafts in the Nineteenth Century: A Note," *Middle East Studies* 37, no. 3 (July 2001).

17. *The Persian Carpet* published by Duckworth in 1953. The role of carpet connoisseurs was not limited to research and publication on the topic of Persian carpets; they were also involved in carpet production, trade, and circulation. Many Oriental carpet connoisseurs became involved in the establishment of the carpet industry in Iran.

18. In one of his letters, he writes, "I think that I told you that the Company had acquired the business of Fritz & LaRue, New York. Since then further absorptions have taken place, which will make the OCM a £1,000,0000 concern. We have bought the business of P. De Andria & Co., Rug brokers, Constantinople; N. Castelli & Brothers, New York; and the Austro Oriental Trading Co. of Vienna and Berlin. The first two of these were about to form a company to fight the OCM, and as they were both very wealthy concerns, they might have done us a good deal of damage. Our board,

therefore, decided to come to terms with them, which was done finally about two months ago." *The Persian Carpet* Letters from Tehran, published by Duckworth in 1953, November 6, 1911.

19. Dyestuff along with sugar and tea were some of the colonial goods imported to Iran by the British. For more information, see Wright, *The English Amongst the Persians*, 101.

20. Nicolas Fokker, *Persian and Other Oriental Carpets for Today* (London: Lewis, Allen and Unwin, 1973), 32.

21. Ibid.

22. George Griffin Lewis, *The Practical Book of Oriental Rugs* (J.B. Lippincott Company, 1913 [scanned from original in 2011]), 77.

23. John Kimberly Mumford, *Oriental Rugs* (Charles Scribner's Sons, 1900), 254.

24. Ibid., 148.

25. E. Gans-Ruedin, *Connaissance du Tapis* (Paris: Vilo, 1971), 22.

26. Emmett Eiland, *Oriental Rugs Today* (Berkeley, CA: Berkeley Hills Books, 2003), 19.

27. Deborah Cohen, *Household Gods* (New Haven, CT: Yale University Press, 2006), x.

28. Ibid.

29. Ibid., 2.

30. Elaine Fleetwood, *The Ideas in Things, Fugitive Meaning in the Victorian Novel* (Chicago: The University of Chicago Press, 2006), 79.

31. See Amy Kaplan, *Cultures of United States Imperialism* (Durham: Duke University Press, 1994).

32. Alison Blunt and Robyn Dowling, *Home*, (New York and London: Routledge, 2006), 145–146.

33. Laura Marks, *Enfoldment and Infinity. An Islamic Genealogy of New Media Art* (Boston: The MIT Press, 2010), 54.

34. Anne McClintock, *Imperial Leather, Race, Gender and Sexuality in the Colonial Contest* (New York and London: Routledge, 1995), 208.

35. Ibid.

36. Ibid., 9.

37. For an extensive analysis of the specific discourse of Orientalism vis-à-vis Iran, see Minoo Moallem, *Between Warrior Brother and Veiled Sister: Islamic Fundamentalism and the Politics of Patriarchy* (Berkeley: University of California Press, 2005).

38. *Jensiat* refers to two things, one is women's sexual difference and the second is women as commodities. The convergence of these two concepts makes domesticity and docility part and parcel of the modernization of patriarchy in Iran.

39. Cited by Samuel Weber, *Targets of Opportunity: On the Militarization of Thinking* (New York: Fordham University Press, 2005), 109.

40. S.G.W. Benjamin, *Persia and the Persians* (London, 1887), 423. Cited by A. Seyf, "Carpet Manufacturers of Iran in the Nineteenth Century," *Middle Eastern Studies* 26, no. 2 (1990): 204–213.

41. The newspaper *Shafaq-e Sorkh* (Red Dawn) was published between 1922 and 1935 in Iran.

42. As I have illustrated elsewhere, the Orientalist discourse vis-à-vis Persia constructed Iranian women as lazy, uneducated, obsessed with sex and food, and not suited to be good mothers. For more information, see Moallem, *Between Warrior Brother and Veiled Sister.*

43. "Girls Sold to Slavery," *The Daily Mail,* April 23, 1928.

44. Ibid.

45. Griffin Lewis, *The Practical Book of Oriental Rugs,* 88.

46. Cecil Edwards, *The Persian Carpet* (Hanson, NJ: Buckworth Publications, 1983[1953]), 51.

47. Chow, *Writing Diaspora,* 44.

48. Christine Delphy, "Pour un *f*éminism matérialist," *Nouvelle Questions Féministes* 2, (October 1981).

49. McClintock, *Imperial Leather.*

50. Michel Foucault, *Discipline and Punish: The Birth of the Prison* (New York: Vintage Books Editions, 1979), 201.

51. The development of an urban carpet industry in Iran started in the Safavid era with the production of very expensive carpets. According to carpet connoisseurs, Safavid court carpets reflect an urban aesthetic made of wool, cotton, and silk with a higher knot density and elaborate pictorial designs (Leonard M. Helfgott, *Production and Trade: The Persian Carpet Industry* (Washington, DC: Smithsonian Institution, 1994)). The economic decline of Safavid carpets is attributed to the historical events following the Afghan invasions of Iran in 1722.

52. From the poem *Liberty,* translated by M. Alexandrian, published in Caroun.com.

53. Colin Campbell, *The Romantic Ethic and The Spirit of Modern Consumerism* (Malden, MA: Wiley-Blackwell, 1987), 204.

54. Plotz notes, "Morris like Arendt, indicts empathy because it operates as a replacement for other, more political sorts of engagement." John Plotz, *Portable Property, Victorian Culture on The Move* (Princeton, NJ: Princeton University Press, 2008), 152.

55. According to Clara C. Rice, Mary Rebecca Stewart Bird was the daughter of a missionary and worked in an Armenian hospital without being a doctor or a nurse. She lived near Julfa and Isphahan. She was in Iran in from the late nineteenth century until 1903, and then went back again in 1911. Cited by Carla C. Rice, *Mary Bird in Persia* (London: Church Missionary Society, 1916), 3.

56. Many feminist or gender-based writings on carpet weavers focus on the exploitative systems within which women weavers are located from global capitalism to classic patriarchy representing pre-modern and religious patriarchy to modern secular patriarchy. While this literature sheds light on the working condition of rural and home-based economies, they have less to do with weaving as cultural capital, the place of women entrepreneurs, or the gendered division of labor within small- and medium-sized workshops. The lack of a transnational and intersectional perspective in this literature leaves a wide opening for a literature that is bringing issues of gender into conversation with class, ethnicity, location, and uneven access

to knowledge of weaving or networking. See among others, Zohreh Ghvamshadi, "The Linkage Between Iranian Patriarchy and the Informal Economy in Maintaining Women's Subordinate Roles in Home-Based Carpet Production," *Women's Studies International Forum* 18, no. 2 (1995): 135–151; Zahra Karimi, *The Effects of International Trade on Gender Inequality: Women Carpet Weavers of Iran.* Working Paper Number 540, The Levy Economics Institute 2008.

57. Kristie Ball and Laureen Snider, eds., *The Surveillance–Industrial Complex: A Political Economy of Surveillance* (New York: Routledge, 2013).

58. No author, *The Carpet Book* (London: Waring and Gillow, 1910), 3.

59. Colette Guillaumin, "Pratique du Pouvoir et idée de Nature (2) Le Discours de La Nature," *Nouvelles Questions Féministes* 3 (Mai, 1978).

60. For examples, see "The Carpet Weaver of Shiraz" by Steve Inskeep for NPR, February 13, 2016, which intended to answer the question of what the lifting economic sanctions against Iran might mean for Zarafshan, a tribal carpet weaver who asks rich people to buy her carpets (www.npr.org/sections/parallels/2016/02/13/466538150/the-carpet-weaver-of-shiraz). In a number of writings on the US embargo, the consideration for poor, rural loom workers is emphasized. See, Eric Pummer, writes "President Clinton lifted the embargo in 2000 before leaving the office, in consideration of the often poor, rural loom workers who produce them," *The Daily Dose*, December 10, 2013. Also, see, Thomas Erdbrink, "The Persian Rug May Not Be Long for This World," *The New York Times*, May 26, 2016.

61. Lori Merish, Sentimental Materialism. ibid, p.1.

62. Jean Baudrillard, *The Consumer Society: Myths and Structures* (London: Sage Publications, 1998), 13.

4

NATION AS COMMODITY

Figure 4.1 **Consuming Persia**
Photographed by Minoo Moallem

"The Persian carpet is the result of passion and knowledge." Interview with a carpet entrepreneur, Tehran, July 2015

Honar nazd-e Iranian ast o bas (Art is only in possession of Iranians). From The Epic of Kings by Iranian poet Ferdowsi

As I explained in prior chapters, while the history of the carpet as an object goes beyond the framework of this book, the genealogy of the carpet as a commodity links not only with colonial modernity but also with the formation of a modern nation-state in Iran. Also, as Benedict Anderson notes, nations as imagined communities are modern inventions. This process of invention of the nation includes both the empire and the state's institutions investing value in the images, icons, tropes, material objects, and ideas of the nation. In this chapter, I argue two things: first, nations are commodities produced and reproduced through mass-mediated and commercial cultures, and second, nations are not only imagined communities but also affective communities.

Since colonial modernity, nations have become tangible through commodity culture, which makes it possible for nations as well as national identities and subjectivities to demand visibility and create affective communities that materialize through commodity circulation and consumer culture. Thus, while nations are imagined communities, they are also commodities that are produced in the context of colonial modernity and the transnationalization of capital, labor, and systems of representation. The nation as a commodity is also a mobile entity with the capacity to move through imperiality, vernacularization, and nationalism, thus creating continuity, connection, and portability. In Rassam Arabzadeh's words carpets are "woven from the Warps of emotion and the wefts of reflection, Persian rugs are thought of as an expanse extended for the people of this country to manifest their artistic talents, this way to put their tastes to the test."[1]

As I explain in the Introduction, while Iran was not directly colonized, it was still controlled by trade and commodities, or informal empire. British formal and informal control of the Persian carpet industry in Iran from the late nineteenth century through the twentieth, via both trade treaties as well as the settlement of factories in various parts of Iran under both the Qajar and Pahlavi rules, show the colonial relations that were established through commodity circulation. The Qajar dynasty's desire for European modernity, especially foreign trade, opened up space for the European control of imports and exports in Iran. Iranian factories and workshops gradually stopped producing cotton and silk, among other commodities, because of the competition from the colonies of the British Empire. Instead, the Persian carpet industry started developing to respond to the increasing demand for Persian carpets by Europeans, especially in Britain, and the United States.

The carpet industry transformed after the establishment of a modern nation-state through the British-assisted coup d'etat of Reza Shah, and continued with the US supported coup d'etat of 1953, following the Iranian Revolution of 1979 and the establishment of the Islamic Republic. These transformations create complex relations between capital and culture, resulting in a discursive shift from the Persian carpet as a commodity from Persia to the Persian carpet as a national commodity displaying both the unity and diversity of the Iranian nation. This discursive and institutional shift took place gradually and slowly, involving local, national, and transnational elite as well as masses of Persian carpet consumers. This process was not unilateral from the top down or from the empire to semi-colonies, but involved different discourses, multiple institutions, and numerous social agents. In this context, I track the rise of the Persian carpet as a national commodity with the growth of commodity culture and in the context of the close association of nations with their commodities.

Becoming a Carpet Nation

Given the vast influence of the British Empire in Iran, carpets and oil were mapped out as the two primary commodities characterizing Iran. As I stated in the previous chapter, British colonial maps from the early twentieth century provide compelling evidence for the visual charting of the oil-producing regions of Iran as well as the carpet-producing areas. The building of the Iranian railroad was also critical in the circulation of both oil and the carpet.[2] The mobility of trains, airplanes, and cars was thus incorporated in the movement of the carpet. The material relations of progress were indeed established not only through the mobility of technology but also through the mobility of commodities.

Before the Bolshevik uprising, Russia competed with the British over influence in Iran given Iran's strategic position and northern border with the Russian Empire. This event led to a period of collaboration before World War I. However, due to the Bolshevik revolution and renunciation of the 1907 Agreement, as well as continuing hostilities between the British and the Soviets, Britain established an absolute hegemony in Iran. Two events influenced this process: one was the failure of the Anglo-Persian agreement of 1919[3] and the other was the backing of the 1921 Coup d'état of Reza Khan. The Soviets remained concerned about Iran and continued their influence by supporting socialist ideas and movements in Iran. At this point, the British Empire controlled both the oil and carpet industries. The Anglo-Iranian Company owned the oil resources, and various British-owned carpet companies controlled the carpet industry. These transformations not only changed the Iranian export economy but also altered the spatial location of labor by establishing urban carpet factories along with small and medium-size workshops while expanding household production. As argued by Marx,

> Not only do the objective conditions change in the act of reproduction, e.g. the village becomes a town, the wilderness a cleaned field etc., but the producers change, too, in that they bring out new qualities in themselves,

develop themselves in production, transform themselves, develop new powers and ideas, new modes of discourse, new needs and new language.[4]

The carpets were mostly exported to the United States, London, Istanbul, Germany, and Austria. According to an Iranian Foreign Ministry document from 1936, more than half of the Iranian carpets were exported to the United States.

The first major carpet exhibition in the United States was in 1893 in Chicago, where Persian carpets had their Pavilion. As I showed in Chapter 2, through the

آمارکل صادرات فرش ایران درآبان ماه ۱۳۱۵

صادرات شهرهای ایران

مبلغ بریال	عده جوازهای صادره	مرکز صادرکننده	نمره ترتیب
۲۷۰۰۱۰۰	۳۳	سلطان آباد	۱
۲۵۰۱۶۱۶	۴۳	تبریز	۲
۲۲۰۸۷۳۸	۶۶	طهران	۳
۱۷۱۷۳۷۳	۲۱	کرمان	۴
۱۷۳۷۱۶۶	۳۳	همدان	۵
۱۴۴۱۴۹۳	۴۴	مشهد	۶
۳۰۴۲۲۸	۱۱	شیراز	۷
۱۲۷۱۱۶۷۴	۲۰۹		

صادرات فرش ایران بهریک از ممالک دنیا

مبلغ بریال	مرکز	نمره ترتیب
۵۱۰۳۳۵۳	امریکا	۱
۳۳۲۴۸۷۸	لندن	۲
۱۰۴۸۷۵۰	ترکیه	۳
۷۷۱۳۶۰	آلمان	۴
۷۷۳۰۷۷	اطریش	۵
۴۰۵۰۸۵	عراق	۶
۲۸۱۰۷۳	چکوسلواکی	۷
۲۱۸۸۴۹	هندوستان	۸
۲۴۴۰۱۱	سوریه	۹
۱۲۲۵۹۲۰	مصر	۱۰
۱۰۳۵۲۱	کانادا	۱۱
۵۲۲۵	سوئد	۱۲
۳۸۷۱۲	عربستان	۱۳
۳۸۳۳۶	سوییس	۱۴

Figure 4.2 **Export of the Carpet. The carpet export in 1936. The US and London are listed as first and second on the list**

در احصائیه که راجع به صادرات کل قالی ایران و صادرات قالی به امریکا در ظرف
پانزده سال اخیر رتبه و تقدیم شده است چند چیز دیده می شود

۱ ـ اهمیت فوق العاده بازرهای امریکا در تجارت قالی ایران (تقریباً با
نصف کلیه صادرات فرش به امریکا ارائه است)

۲ ـ تنزل صادرات قالی ایران به امریکا در سنوات اخیره مخصوصاً در
سال ۱۳۱۳

۳ ـ تنزل فاحش صادرات قالی های پشمی جوهری در چند سال خیر نسبت
به سنوات ۱۳۲ و ۱۳۰۸ که مطابق با (۱۱۲۸/۲۹ و ۱۲۹/۳۰ اسمی
است)

۴ ـ ثبات نسبی صادرات قالی های پشمی رنگ ثابت به امریکا

صادرات قالی که در پانزده سال اخیر روی هم رفته قریب ۳۰ درصد صادرات کل مملکت
راتشکیل داده و صد و پنجاه هزار نفر ایرانی از این ممر اعاشه میکنند درتجارت خارجی
ایران حائز اهمیت مخصوص است و حفظ بازرهای مملکتی مثل امریکا
که تا حدود و زخر بیدار نصف صادرات کل قالی ایران بوده است درسیا ست اقتصادی
ایران در درجه اول اهمیت واقع شده و بها یدکذاشت تجارت قالی سیر قهقرائی تی را
که در چند سال اخیر بر اثر بحران اقتصادی دینامعلسه پیدا کرده ادامه دهد
صادرات قالی های پشمی رنگ ثابت نسبت به قالی های جوهری تنزل کمتری
نشان میدهد و دلیل آن این است قطع نظر از اینکه قالی های پشمی رنگ ثابت در دنیا
بیشتر طالب دارد و قالی های و جوهری یه عکس از شهرت فرش ایرا نکاسته و
به نسبا رت آن لطمه وارد میکند درسند و اینکه مصادف با بحران اقتصادی شده مقدار
زیادی قالی های قدیم و نفیس از مملکت خارج شده و از این راه لطمه بزرگی به
ثروت ملی ایران وارد آمده است

Figure 4.3 **A document from the Iranian Foreign Ministry emphasizing the importance of carpet export to the United States in 1928 and 1929.**

collection and exhibition of objects in museums, world's fairs, and world exhibitions, commodities, people, and territories gradually merged with each other, creating a basis for the establishment of nation-states. The idea of the nation as a bounded identity coincided with the emergence of national commodities. The nation started to be defined not only as an imagined community but as a commodity to be exhibited and displayed, collapsing the nation with its commodities and further orienting the nation towards unification and cohesion. The transformation of imperial commodity culture to national commodity culture relied heavily on the value invested in objects of the past and commodities of the present. Commodities provided a material evidence for the immutability of the nation. Questions of citizenship and consumption became integrally connected with each other.

Slowly but surely, the Persian carpet developed into a vital national commodity and a site of middle-class consumption both in Iran and transnationally. The desire for carpets coincided with the transformation of labor in two forms: the continuation of informal labor within the household and the expansion of workshop and factory carpet weaving. According to Helfgott, post-1875 wage labor represented a new form of productive relationship in Iran, and by the turn of the twentieth century, hand-knotted carpets became Iran's main export to the West.[5] The carpet also became an integral part of the Iranian home culture of consumption.[6] In Iran, affective nationalism was key in the commodification of Persian carpets.

The homing of the domestic space was built around the spatial imaginary of home, not as a bounded place, but as going between the private and the public, the house and the national territorial imagination, the homeland and the diaspora. The transformation of the notion of home in the early twentieth century created a lot of confusion in the Iranian urban culture, where the reference to home included a variety of spatial and symbolic metaphors including *manzel* (the household as well as the wife and children), *khaneh* (the house), *andarooni* (the private and feminized space physically and symbolically), and *birooni* (the opposite of *andarooni*, referring to the private and masculinized space). These concepts sometimes depicted gendered spaces and at other times gender relations. Commodities displaying Iranian-ness, such as Persian carpets, made it possible for the Iranian home and Iran as a homeland to converge with each other through the consumption of both modern appliances made in the West and commodities displaying national Iranian-ness. The formation of an authentic Iranian culture and the durability and uniqueness of Persian carpets as an ancient and timeless craft made a primordial claim on national culture as eternal and everlasting.[7] This discursive shift changed power relations, and after World War I, the industry was taken over gradually by Iranian traders, entrepreneurs, and mediators—mostly the male patriarchal elite—and through the consolidation of the institution of the Iranian bazaar. In the late 1940s and early 1950s, Persian carpets became the top exported commodity after oil. The carpet industry remained largely invested in exporting the carpet to the West until the revolution of 1979, the US embargo, and the carpet industry's reinvestment in domestic and diasporic consumption directed exports to other parts of the world, including the Gulf region.[8]

The Urbanites, the Rural, and the Nomadic: Ethnicization of the Nation and the Institution of the Bazaar

"The touch of Kerman carpet: the more you step on it, the more beautiful it will become."

Popular saying

The display of commodities in world's fairs and museums made it possible for various nations to represent themselves as commodities on a global stage. It also provided space for nation-states to enter global networks of productive consumption through national products. This process was not a simple and unilateral one, but included a complex web of agents and mediators at the local, national, and global levels. Given that Iran is a multiethnic and multi-religion country, the diversity of ethnic experiences was inserted into the unity of the nation through commodities. Carpets were the best vehicles for resolving the contradiction between the nation as both unified and divided. These contradictions became a site of conflict and antagonism after the Reza Shah coup d'etat of 1921 and the centralization of the state in the name of the nation. Many Kurds, Turks, Arabs, Lurs, and Beluchs, along with some tribal leaders and religious minority traders, became anxious about a centralized dictatorship that relied on the notion of the Aryan race and the dominance of Farsi as the formal language. Reza Shah, along with his state elite, also started to confiscate land, claiming ownership of some of the most prosperous parts of Iran and devastating many tribe leaders and urban landowners. Yet, as Helfgott notes, "The European fascination with primitive cultures, for humans 'in the state of nature' created a demand for old village and nomadic rugs."[9]

In the 1920s, after oil, Persian carpets were Iran's second largest foreign currency. The modernizing nation-state, and its apparatus became more and more involved in Persian carpet's trade. As stated by Martin Rudner, the Persian carpet industry went through two transformations: first was the state's investment in the carpet industry and its quality assurance, and second was the expansion of a domestic market controlled by the new administrative and bureaucratic local elite and the emergent national elite's desire for carpets.[10] The modernizing nation-state started to invest in the production of a homogenized national identity and carpets became a material site of both homogenization and ethnicization.

In this context, ethnicity, as Rey Chow argues, is defined within the context of global capitalism, not outside of it. She writes, "*To be ethnic is to protest*—but perhaps less for the actual emancipation of any kind than for benefits of world-wide visibility, currency, and circulation."[11] The ethnicization of the carpet and its distinction based on design, color, and quality facilitated the inclusion of ethnic minorities. This process involved the distinction of the carpets based on urban, rural, and tribal makeups. For example, the carpets' design, style, color, and weaving qualities distinguished Tabriz-made carpets from Kurdish or Tukeman carpets and brought them all under a unified national commodity as the signifier of the Iranian nation. This process also enabled local entrepreneurs to access regional and cosmopolitan networks to control their communities, especially in the tribal and rural areas. This form of scrutiny reinforced paternalistic and patriarchal relations. Men became mostly involved in the ownership of the urban factories and workshops that had a concentration of male workers. In more rural and tribal areas, men also became the primary mediating agent as the head of the households. As I have argued, the modernization of patriarchy did not eliminate unequal gender relations but established the institution of family as a unit of consumption, with men as providers and heads of the family and women as housewives. Furthermore, the housewifization of women went hand in hand with the rise of consumerism.[12] This shift from the household as a unit of production to a unit of consumption had catastrophic consequences for rural and tribal women who were substantially involved in agriculture and craftwork.

As opposed to oil and its nationalization in the 1950s by the nationalist elite of Dr. Mossadagh's administration, the transfer of the power and ownership of the Persian carpet industry from the British to the Iranian elite took place gradually. In 1936, the government established *Sherkat sahami Farsh* Iran, or the Iranian Carpet Company to be in charge of regulating the production and sales of the carpets; however, the company's monopoly was suspended in 1938 and the carpet was again open to independent firms.[13] In this context, the Iranian bazaar played a significant role in governing and taking over the trade, though the carpet trade remained broadly transnational. The carpet industry involved many traders from religious minorities in Iran, including Iranian Jews and Armenians who had contact with traders in other parts of the world. As for the Iranian bazaar, while most of the time Orientalist scholarship refers to it either as a mysterious, irrational, and traditional, bounded space, or as a preexisting object and timeless space, these depictions cannot explain the significance of the bazaar in the life of Persian carpets.

The bazaar is a gendered local, trans-local, and transnational network of economic and cultural relations of exchange and circulation of commodities. The bazaar can be defined as a socio-economic site of modernity, in Nitasha Kaul's words.[14] One of the most significant aspects of the bazaar is its mediation not only between the local, the national, and the transnational but also between the formal and informal sites of production, exchange, and circulation. As Kajri Jain notes in the case of India, the bazaar is an economic and cultural space, a trans-vernacular network of trade and a cyclic event that is repeated through a web of relationships extending beyond and between individual sites.[15] Most scholarship in Iranian and Middle Eastern studies are still depicting the bazaar in essentializing terms and as a site of trade representing the traditional and religious elite of traders and entrepreneurs. For example, in depicting the Isfahan bazaar, Velashani et al. write, "The inner built space of Iran's cities bazaars is artistically and technically rich as well as mysterious; it is both inviting and hindering, cautious and conservative."[16]

Furthermore, the state's patterns of intervention emphasized the carpet as both a multiethnic national commodity and a traditional authentic craft. For example, while the demand for mixed-design carpets or carpets that appealed aesthetically to the Euro-American export-oriented industry were dominant, a return to what is called neo-classical carpet design emphasizing distinct local characteristic flourished after the establishment of the modern nation-state.[17] The desire to be included in the modern "family of nations" and yet have a distinct identity for a multiethnic country like Iran was satisfied through what Canclini calls "symbolic consumption," as it provided the basis for shared identities.[18] Jila Rassam Arabzadeh, a carpet exporter, notes that "The Persian carpet is like the Iranian flag, known all over the world. Let our flag fly."[19] The market, including the bazaar, insisted in the preservation of the informal organization of weaving and the institution of the patriarchal family, since that unit was more efficient, less expensive, and more susceptible to the control of the local middlemen.

The *Sherkat* came under the control of the Ministry of *Jihad sazandegi* (reconstruction crusade) after the fall of the Pahlavi regime and the Iranian revolution of 1979, when the goal of creating jobs in the realm of agriculture became an important focus of this foundation. The state's reinvestment in the carpet industry regardless of the US embargo and its devastating impact on the carpet industry was manifold. However, redirecting the carpet production towards Iranian consumers both in Iran and in the diaspora as well as European, East Asian countries, and the Gulf States was crucial in the continued production of the carpets. In this context, new meanings were inscribed on the carpet as a national commodity.

Since the Iranian revolution and the establishment of the Islamic Republic, and with the mass dislocation of Iranians from Iran in the post-revolutionary era, many changes have taken place in the Persian carpet industry. First of all, while Iranian Jews and Armenians were traditionally invested in the carpet trade, many of them left Iran after the establishment of the Islamic Republic and settled in New York or Los Angeles as carpet dealers and traders. The history of the establishment of carpet dealers in New York and Los Angeles goes back to the early twentieth century, when a few carpet and antique dealers of Iranian Armenian and Iranians Jewish background established their trade in these locations. According to one of the dealers, these entrepreneurs started to invest value in some carpets as having a better design or better quality than others, making them more popular among diasporic communities.[20]

Since 2000, the Islamic Republic has reinvested in the carpet industry as a national commodity. In 2003 and within the context of the Ministry of Industries, Mines and Commerce, the Iran National Carpet Center was established as a non-governmental organization to coordinate and synchronize all aspects of production and marketing of Iranian handwoven carpets, especially in promoting and expanding global markets.[21] In collaboration with the Kish Trade Promotion Center, they have been organizing The Kish Island Handmade Carpet International Exhibition since 2002.[22]

Talie Abad is a microcosm of how carpet production and circulation works. As I recounted in the previous chapter, carpet weaving, along with shepherding and drug trafficking, are the main modes of subsistence in the village. Most weavers are women, while both men and women function as foremen, with women mostly mediating the labor. Mr. Aliakbar is the village middleman between the consumers, the bazaar, and the weavers. His house is filled with piles of carpets produced in the village. He provides the women weavers with what they need to weave the carpet, mostly the loom and the yarn. He frequently takes the carpets to the Nain, Kashan, or Isfahan bazaar and sells them to carpet merchants, who are very cautious about who their connection with the village is.

The bazaar is a gendered space, and most bazaaris and middlemen are men. Women are either weavers or, if they have an extra room in their houses, like Zahra, they hire other women to weave carpets. While some of those women themselves weave the carpets, as we saw in the previous chapter, they are also in charge of organizing and managing the labor along with their household work, including cooking, cleaning, and taking care of children and elders.

Figure 4.4 **Carpet in the Bazaar**
Alexander Mazurkevich/Shutterstock.com

Women are also in charge of making cheese, yogurt, or other dairy-based products. Tahereh, who has a little store in the village, is one of them. Her house has two extra rooms, and she can set up the looms and hire other women to weave for her. She has less time to weave the carpet herself, but as a shopkeeper she has a broad network of women weavers. She is also familiar with the trade and can negotiate a better deal with the village middlemen. She tells me that occasionally she works with another entrepreneur who drops by and orders a few carpets. The network of mediators, household entrepreneurs, and weavers are entangled with each other and involve both formal and informal modes of operation. These networks are both connected to the bazaar and function independently whenever possible.

The Rise of the Urban Heteronormative Family as a Site of Consumption

"Women appreciate and remember art more often, and this should be the case when it comes to the carpets, but if men get interested, it is because of the carpet value. They pay attention to the carpet because of its value."

Interview with carpet-company owner
Mr. Hakimi, San Francisco, 2011

With the modernization and Westernization of Iran after the coup d' état of Reza Khan in 1921 and the establishment of the Pahlavi regime in 1925, the institution of the nuclear family with an investment in reproductive heterosexuality gradually replaced more extended forms of family. Many scholars have argued that there is a relationship between the rise of industrial capitalism and the emergence of domesticity in the bourgeois interior. According to Benjamin, the bourgeois interior was intimately linked with exploitation, injustice, and capitalist values of property and ownership.[23] Also, the modern family became a unit of consumption with various new household appliances and consumer goods targeted for women as housewives. Even with the entrance of women into more feminized segments of the labor market, including teaching, nursing, and other forms of service, the household continued to be a site of consumption for modern women. As for Persian carpets, while their export remained central and modern housing, especially apartments, relied on importing machine-made rugs, handmade carpets continued to be a major component of urban middle-class and upper-middle-class furniture.

In this context, even though the Persian carpet industry relied heavily on the work of masses of women and children, the advertisements targeting consumers depicted women mostly in two different ways: either as the carpet

Figure 4.5 **Eroticizing the Carpet**
t-lorien/Vetta/Getty Images

itself or as the housewives and beneficiaries of the comfort and beauty of the carpet. In the women-as-carpets ads, the woman's body is coupled with the carpet to convey the message that women's bodies and carpets are similar, if not the same.

Men continued to occupy the role of owners and buyers of the carpets.

The juxtaposition of carpets with women reveals the commodification of women's bodies along with carpets. The spectacle of labor, as I argued in the previous chapter, represented through the images of tribal and rural women, was accompanied with the spectacle of leisure, including urban women enjoying the comfort of the carpets at home. These two spectacles complement each other by constructing women's emotional labor in the domestic sphere (cooking, cleaning, caring for children and older people) as non-work and non-value. Although gender is produced through discursive forces, as various feminist scholars argue, it is maintained and reproduced through spatial elements, including objects of consumption. In this context, gender is manufactured in everyday life via consumerism.[24] The stylization of the interior has a lot to do with gender meanings and gender identities. Notions of comfort, coziness, and a private haven from the public all rely on the construction of the home and its commodities.[25] In many ads, the representation of a comfortable home follows the idea of men as providers and owners of the carpet, while women and children are its consumers. The construction of home as a heteronormative space is also part of this gendering of the home space.

The Carpet as the Nation and the Nation as the Carpet

The process of national formation cannot be separated from the transnational context of colonial modernity, and the invention of nations as characterized by their internal cultural differences. A significant aspect of this formation is defined by commodity culture and the way in which each nation is constructed and displayed through its commodities. National commodities displayed nations as authentic and primordial. This notion of representing cultural authenticity and essence in national commodities was invented by nation-states as they started to bring the nation into the temporality of modernity, development, and progress. The notion of cultural authenticity was fabricated and materialized through commodities.

As I showed in the first chapter, the notion of cultural authenticity was first an invention of Orientalist paintings and photography that depicted Persian carpets as a site of Persian-ness. Many photographic images during the Qajar era (1794–1925), including photographs by Antoin Sevruguin (the son of the Georgian-Armenian diplomat), represent Qajar women sitting or posing on a Persian carpet. Similarly, there are many vintage photographs depicting women and the carpet.

While commodities are essential components of the interior, the relationship between subjects and commodities is extremely meaningful given that in a consumerist society, signs of class, race, or gender are not apparent from the ownership of a product but from the relationships subjects have with the commodities. For example, the male elite's identification with the carpet as a signifier of class and ethnic distinction, family prestige, and Iranian identity is reflected not only in those who own the carpet but also by the male bazaar elite who controlled the networks of middlemen and weavers as they gradually managed to block Euro-American control of the carpet industry.

In this case, national identity is both identification with the nation as a commodity as well as a set of material practices and objects that constitute the individual as a national subject. The nationalization of commodities and commodification of the nation as projects of modernization in Iran were integral to the process of nation building. This process involves several deliberations, including the investment of the state in image production and image circulation. This system started with the Qajar dynasty and continued with the consumerism of the Pahlavi era. The Qajar dynasty brought tradition into the temporality of modernity, including the state sponsorship of pictorial carpets. Many carpets woven during the Qajar era are tableau vivant depicting the political leaders from various parts of the world or displaying different nations. (For an insightful analysis of a few examples of these carpets see: Charles Kurzman, "Weaving Iran Into The Tree of Nations" *Int. J. Middle East Stud.* 37 (2005), 137–166.)

Figure 4.6 **Depicting the United States with the Figure of a Native American**
Photographed by Minoo Moallem

For example, the carpet depicted in the photo from the early twentieth century, and currently held at the Carpet Museum of Tehran, represents a number of nations, including the United States through the figure of a Native American.

This process, in the later stages, distinguished the Persian carpet as an authentic site of tradition. However, in the 1970s, under the Pahlavi regime and after the establishment of the Carpet Museum of Tehran, the carpet moved from the space of tradition to the space of modern museums. After the Iranian revolution of 1979, the carpet again became a hybrid site of convergence between modern painting and carpet weaving.

The Carpet Museum of Tehran is more ambiguous than the Oriental or Islamic art sections of European or American museums, where history is monumentalized and fixed in time through the narratives of colonial modernity and its Islamic Others. The museum itself is a replica of a carpet loom, it obscures the lived experience of the carpet by making it into a static national monument. The museum's proximity to various sites of production on the one hand, and its status as a site of the national heritage and under state protection, on the other, have influenced how the carpets are displayed. Many precious carpets from different eras are displayed next to each other with no explanatory text, except for the year of their fabrication and, in very few instances, the name of the well-known male carpet-weaving master. The museum employees are instructed to not talk to the visitors. During one of my visits to the museum, one of the employees who found out about my interest in studying the carpets started to speak to me about the carpets, but made sure I understood that he could not

walk and talk with me or draw any attention to our conversation. He kept showing up as I was moving through the exhibition to give me some information
about a particular carpet. I realized that as a national commodity, any access to
the sites and networks of production, circulation, and display had to be moni-
tored. The displacement of some of the carpets from the palaces of the ancien
régime as a decorative furniture item to their emplacement in the museum,
removed from the everyday temporality of weaving and consuming, turn the
carpet into an eternal abstraction of national history. The de-commodification
of the carpet in this case and its placement in the time of the nation makes the
museum space more ambiguous given the proximity of the museum to the production, exchange, and consumption sites.

Re-orienting the Look and Mass Consumption of the Nation

The Iranian revolution of 1979 provided momentum for modernist Iranian artists, film directors, and producers to turn the modernist/modernizing high-art
gaze of the Pahlavi era inward, in an aesthetically revisionist yet nostalgic political move. The US embargo against Iranian commodities, especially the Persian
carpet, also made certain commodities a site of national resistance and affective
speculation. This scopic shift displayed an intense desire and curiosity for the
pleasures of looking at "things Persian or Iranian," including the Persian carpet, among other commodities, not only as a craft but as art, bringing high art
and popular art into the same frame of reference. This aesthetic move brought
the carpet to the realm of belonging and identity as a sign of Iranian-ness,
investing new symbolic value in what was once "Orientalia" in nineteenth- and
twentieth-century European and American writings, as I discussed in Chapter 2.
The re-appropriation of the carpet as an image previously separating subjects
from objects, and re-making it into the nation itself (including both subjects
and material objects), was the beginning of a shift that moved the carpet out of
its commodity state and into the national art realm. This process created a new
field of power providing a shared cultural expression for consuming publics, or
a new notion of sociality that included both urban and rural classes as well as
emplaced and displaced citizen-subjects.

The brilliant Iranian director Ali Hatami in his 1984 movie *Kamalulmoulk*
puts this moment on view. As a feature film, it depicts the life and work of
Kamalulmoulk, who was one of the first Iranian modernist painters. He master-
fully mixed modernist perspectivism with naturalist and realist painting themes
and techniques and Iranian motifs, in addition to making copies of European
paintings by well-known European artists, as well as using modernist technics
of painting in his depiction of Iranian spaces. In the early twentieth century, he
was invited to the court of Naseeruddin Shah Qajar, where he painted a portrait

of the Shah as well as his entourage, European visitors, and various scenes of the Golestan Palais. Naseeruddin Shah Qajar (1831–1896), well known for his passion for modern technologies of photography, film, and painting, supported Kamalulmoulk to create some of his most famous paintings. However, after the collapse of the Qajar dynasty and the coup d'état of Reza Shah Pahlavi, Kamalulmoulk, who was at that point a constitutionalist, was invited back to the court, this time with the authoritative request from Reza Shah to paint his portray. After refusing to follow the new dictator's order because of health issues, Kamalulmoulk was exiled to a remote rural village in Neyshabour in the Eastern part of Iran.

The film depicts an encounter between Kamalulmoulk and a rural carpet weaver called Master Mohammad, who offers the artist a carpet he was weaving during Kamalulmoulk's exile in the village, out of admiration and respect for the master of modern painting. He asks him to be the first to step on the carpet. In an affective moment, where the economy of the gift and Kamalulmoulk's dislocation from his routine urban, cosmopolitan, and modern perspective makes him look at the carpet in a new light, he is overwhelmed by the beauty of it. Kamalulmoulk declares,

> Ostad Mohammad you are the master and the artist who have created this work of art, you are the one with the talent and creativity. I regret that in my whole life, I never looked at what was underneath my feet, Ostad Mohammad, you are the master, and the masterpiece is yours, not mine.

Perspectivism and vision are central to modernist painting. However, given that the optic eye is invited to look in a particular direction, re-orienting the look requires both the eye and the haptic memory of the hand-knotted carpets. The encounter with the carpet requires the touch of the feet and the body sensation. In common accounts, a good-quality carpet is a carpet that "the more you step on it, the more precious it becomes." Kamalulmoulk's realization in this moment captures the ways in which the most valuable work of art is not in front of a viewer, as the object of one's gaze, but underneath one's feet. The male gaze of the director is joined together with the affirmation of the modern male artist in representing a masculinized moment of national consciousness. Obviously, the female weaver as an artist is expelled from this moment of national recognition.

The film not only exposes a moment of disillusion and distancing from the modernist perspectivism of high art but also directs the spectators' look, along with the national painter's, towards the material objects of everyday life. The film also animates masculinist nationalist affects through the encounter of high art and popular craft, provoking a desire for the nation as both an art and a commodity. In this moment of nationalist affect, the film comments on the modernist distancing of the carpet from its social context and the laboring bodies of rural as well as urban women and children, abstracting it to the level of a national fetish. Both desired and disavowed by the modernist elite and men of the newly emerging middle classes, the Persian carpet becomes a signifier for the timeless co-habitation of tradition and modernity.

This filmic moment of encounter between two artists—both as trans-individual subjects, Kamalulmoulk as a national icon and Ostad Mohammad as representing a network of designers and weavers—hardly fits individualist and modernist notions of the genius artist. The encounter between Kamalulmoulk, the carpet, and its maker epitomizes a moment where the Orientalist and nationalist modes of image-making invest new value in images, as they provide access to the essence of the nation, in this case Iranian-ness. This also gives new value to the carpet in its commodity state, again this time as embodying the nation, both in Iran and in the diaspora. This filmic moment depends on a prior moment of national consciousness in the mid-twentieth century and the involvement of the bazaar elite as they took over the carpet industry from the imperial companies. If the earlier moment was marked by a distinctive sense of social encounter depicted by objects and material things, the later moment depicted in the film refers to a continuous flow of time inhabited by the protagonists as well as the spectators.

As I showed in Chapter 2, the carpet motif in Hollywood movies serves to describe so-called Orientals as different, attaching them to a particular aesthetic that was both imaginary and magical. In Chapter 3, we saw how films are an important component of commercializing and displaying consumerist cultures of domesticity, exoticism, Orientalism, and nationalism. Here they continue to be significant, in the intimate relation between the Iranian film industry and the consumption of the carpet as a signifier of Iranian-ness, as a component of the modern household that depicts cultural origin, indigeneity, and connection to the past.

Carpets as Mnemonic Commodity:
Gabbeh, *Frash-e Irani*, and *Farsh-e bad*

Following the Iranian revolution of 1979, the Islamic republic successfully integrated the working classes, lower-middle classes, and peasantry into consumer culture. Through the establishment of a welfare state, the development of rural areas, and the inclusion of rural and tribal people in the process of citizenship, the Islamic republic enhanced the purchasing power of rural people. This—along with the expansion of media and TV to remote areas—has resulted in rural people investing more in home decoration, including carpets. However, because of the high price of handwoven carpets, machine-made copies have become a decorative component of many rural homes, even in carpet-weaving households. The workers who produce handmade carpets are now buying machine-made ones at cheaper prices.

Since the post Iran-Iraq war in early 2000, the carpet motif has become a central signifier of the Islamic nation in popular visual culture. In addition to movies and TV series where the carpet is used to display Iranian-ness, the carpet museum of Tehran and regular carpet exhibitions in the Kish Islands, as well as in a number of carpet-producing cities, are promoting carpets as a national commodity.

Many movies depict not only the carpet as a decorative national object emphasizing Iranian-ness but also characters who have connections to the carpet industry, including the bazaar. Taking their national importance a step further, a number of movies depict the increased affective investment in the Persian carpet not only as a site of national identity but also as a mnemonic transnational commodity. In this sense, carpets are sites of memory that carry local and national stories across borders. Let me now focus on three movies that depict carpets in this way.

The Color of Life or the Color of Nation?

The film *Gabbeh* (1997), directed by Mohsen Makhmalbaf, gives voice to this low-knotted, colorful carpet, mostly made by nomadic people in Iran, and which sometimes have stories interwoven in them through little figurative characters. Gabbeh in Farsi refers to "something raw or natural, uncut or 'in the rough.'" Gabbeh are the world's best-known coarsely woven Iranian tribal rugs. Traditionally, the knotting and weaving of nomadic carpets are a woman's domain and area of expertise. Many nomadic rugs such as the Gabbeh are almost exclusively knotted for personal use, and often the woman's artisanship are quite apparent in these personal interpretations of their life in art."[26] The film starts when an older man and woman are washing their rug, which portrays the figure of a woman named Gabbeh and a man on a horseback. The old woman asks the female figure on the carpet who she was, and she steps out of the rug to recount her love story with the man on the horse. The film aestheticizes tribal life and rugs through Gabbeh, a young woman who struggles to remember her desire for love as opposed to the life imposed on her by her tribal community. Gabbeh the rug functions as a mnemonic device that tells the story of a multiethnic nation through an unfulfilled romantic love story. The juxtaposition of cinematic naturalism; a quasi-ethnographic depiction of tribal life; a heterosexual marriage between the poetic middle-aged teacher and a young, tribal, poetic woman; and the abjectified and unfulfilled desire for love that is sacrificed for the sake of the community perpetuate the myth of the nation as unified. Through the recurring repetition of "color is life, life is color," in the movie, the nation as the carpet is sexualized, eroticized, and recounted as natural, primordial, and heteronormative.

The film shows women weaving Gabbeh, an act that, in addition to the weaving of the stories in the film, incorporates family, tribal life, and the nation into the carpet's patterns. The story turns to two different endings: one with the girl Gabbeh's claim, "I had the opportunity to escape but did not have the courage to do it." And the second, which depicts Gabbeh escaping with her lover. However, this version of the story ends tragically with the Gabbeh's father shooting his disobedient daughter to teach a lesson to the young women in the village. The textile speaks to the text that is buried in narration of the nation. The carpet as a mnemonic object mirrors modern constructions of the nation either as based on reproductive heteronormativity or as tragic love. The sentimental juxtaposition of two endings, one leading to a conjugal union and the other to the tragic death of Gabbah as she escapes with her lover in the film, display the impossibility of integrating women and tribal communities into the fabric of the nation without sacrificing women as subjects of desire and objects of patriarchal control.[27]

Farsh-e bad *and the Eternal Life of the Nation*

"In my life, I have finally come to realize that material things are valueless, it is the cultural work that has value since it lives even after one's death."

The voice of the Japanese character from the movie

Farsh-e bad, from director Kamal Tabrizi, was made in 2003. The film starts in Japan, in Japanese with Farsi subtitles. Two men are organizing a ceremony to celebrate the cultural relationship between Iran and Japan, and one of the men wants to order a Persian carpet for it. He talks to another man, who promises to order the carpet through his connection with Iranian carpet dealers. The film is set within the historical context of increasing trade relations between Iran and Japan beginning in 2000.[28] As the film progresses, we learn that the younger man, Mr. Makato, is in the Iranian carpet trade and his wife, who has a terminal disease, is designing the carpet for the ceremony. They also have a daughter named Sakura, who develops an interest in Persian carpets through her mother. She tells Sakura that the Persian carpets can recreate nature and natural colors; she sees the possibility of eternal life in the carpet. Sakura's mother's sense of the intersection of life, nature, and art in the carpet design presents the possibility of both remembering and retrieving endless life beyond national borders.

After the death of his wife, Mr. Makato takes Sakura to Isfahan, a major carpet-weaving city and tourist destination, to pick up the carpet he had ordered for the ceremony and that his wife had designed. The carpet becomes a site of cultural exchange between Japan and Iran, but also a place for family affect, as the father and daughter travel to Iran to honor the dream of their deceased wife and mother. They stay with the family of a carpet trader in Iran, where they are exposed to the performance of Iranian culture of hospitality. Soon, however, the audience learns that the carpet had been ordered, but mistakenly was not woven. The Isfahani trader becomes aware of the emotional significance of the carpet for Mr. Makato and his daughter, and with the help of a young boy who works for an urban carpet workshop, organizes everyone so the carpet can be made within 20 days, in time for the ceremony. During this time, Sakura and the boy develop a deep friendship.

In an ethnographic move, the film depicts the process of carpet weaving, and all the rituals before and after a carpet is woven. But it provides only a partial picture of the life of the men and women—including weavers, traders, workshop owners, merchants, and kids—who work in the gendered sections of the carpet industry. This depiction of different actors lacks any representation of class relations and romanticizes Persian rugs as the product of the harmonious collaboration of various social agents in carpet production.

In addition to the collaborative aspect of carpet-making, the film also represents certain rituals performed by weavers once they start to weave a carpet. They begin with one ceremony and finish with another one. As a vital matter, from the moment a carpet is started it carries with it the potential to perform anything from transmitting memories to performing miracles. The time of production is shown as a time in-between the ritual of ascending and descending the carpet from the loom. This temporality does not follow the capitalist logic of a workday or the limit of hours one can work at the loom, but an unlimited working time from the beginning to the end of the carpet's weaving. The movie quickly breaks with this time and moves to another temporality, the temporality of a sublime and beautiful commodity.

The mobility of the carpet consolidates the stability of both family and nation in their eternal life through memory and affects. The film also juxtaposes the collective affects around love, life, and loss in that location with the eternity of the Persian carpets as a national commodity, representing the Iranian nation both materially and symbolically as a valued commodity.

Farsh-e Irani: *Fifteen Directors, One Story*

Farsh-e Irani, or *The Iranian Carpet*, was sponsored by the Persian artnama institution, the semi-private Persian Art Picture Institute that was established in

2004 and functions as a national and global institute for the production and distribution of Iranian films and animation, under the rules and regulation of the Islamic State. This film won the Simurgh prize at the Fajr International Film Festival, which is under the supervision of the Ministry of Culture and Islamic Guidance. The film is thus a product of the state's reinvestment in the carpet industry and the export of Persian carpets as a national commodity. It also relates to the reinvestment in Iranian culture and civilization that led to divisions between the state elite, especially those advocating the "Iranian school" who believed it was time for the state to distance itself from Islam and reinvest in Iranian culture versus those who opposed them.[29] Made in 2007, this omnibus film is composed of 15 short films in the style of documentary fiction that focus on Farsh-e Irani (Iranian carpets) as the material symbol of Iranian unity and diversity. Fifteen prominent directors, 14 men and one woman (well-known director Rakhshan Bani-Etemad), tell a visually alluring story about Iranian carpets as part of the Iranian historical, artistic, and cultural heritage. Each short film has a title and starts with a citation from the director.

The shift from calling the carpets Persian (a nineteenth-century convention associating them with the Persian empire) to Iranian (a national identity invented after the establishment of the modern nation-state in Iran) in the film makes a claim on carpets as a signifier of the essence of Iranian national belonging rather than a material object from the distant past. This cinematic move is consistent with the shift from an Islamic nationalism to an Iranian nationalism. In this film, carpets are denoted an *a priori* site of the infinite and mythical time of the nation. The stories mostly depict women weavers as silent signifiers and focus either on the carpet owners, dealers, and traders, or the carpet itself as an art object and a commodity. Most of these short films depict carpets made by Iranian tribes, including Lurs, Turkomans, and Azerbaijani. One of the main themes in the movie is the distinction between Persian carpets made cheaply in China, India, Egypt, and Pakistan and the authentic Iranian carpets, which reflect the spirit and colorful nature of Iranian tribes. Another theme references the long history of carpets in Iran going back to the Safavid era, and even before Mugul occupation of Iran. Some of the themes that connect the 15 carpets to the nation include carpets as the essence of Iranian spirit (the first carpet by Behrooz Afkhami); carpets as a site of convergence between Iranian poetry, writing, and design (the eleventh carpet by Abbas Kiarostami); carpets as a mobile sacred landscape (the twelfth carpet by Majid Majidi); carpet design as an Iranian art (the second carpet, by Rakhshan Bani Etemad); and finally carpets as capital (the fourth carpet by Jafar Panahi). Here I will focus on just four of the carpets to illustrate how they construct the carpet as a multiethnic and authentic national commodity while concealing gendered aspects of the labor, especially through their representation of women weavers.

I. THE FIRST CARPET: THE IRANIAN SPIRIT IN *FARSH-E ASHAYERI*

"Persian carpet. . . . A world of nuances, full of imagination. . . . Repeating trees, streams, and blossoms. . . . A utopia took from Iranian spirit."

Behrooz Afkhami, the director of *Farsh-e Ashayeri*

The first film visually depicts a group of women from the Bakhtiari tribes (a Southwestern Iranian tribe, and a subgroup of the Lurs) dancing and weaving carpets. However, the voice of the female narrator tells the story of Gholamreza Zolanbari, who was dragged by his father into the trade and export of Bakhtiari carpets. According to the film, Zolanbari got involved in this trade 60 years ago. Thirty thousand weavers, mostly women, according to the film, are now working for him, and so many other thousands, mostly men, work for him washing, dyeing, and completing the carpets. The film positions original tribal carpets that are made by "the youthful and colorful spirit of Bakhtiari" against the fake carpets made cheaply and artificially in China, India, or Pakistan. Traditional Iranian music accompanies the film to involve other senses, in this case, acoustic. The film's construction of authenticity through music, tribal women, and the landscape represents the carpet and the nation as irreplaceable. Though both men and women are represented in this film, men are given access to the ownership of the carpet industry while women are depicted as weavers. Both ethnic difference and gender difference are there as the context within which the male-dominated carpet industry could be recognized. The spirit of the nation is affectively remembered through male power and property, juxtaposed with the sensational depiction of the tribal landscape, women's dancing and weaving, and traditional music.

II. THE FOURTH CARPET: UNTYING THE KNOT—CARPET AS CAPITAL

"Today, over a thousand knots are woven into the texture of a carpet. Tomorrow, they might un-knot our life problems."

Jafar Panahi

Jafar Panahi's film depicts a brother and her mute sister who is taking an old carpet inherited from their parents and made by their grandmother to the bank as collateral for a loan. The film shows a long line of people waiting for their carpets to be assessed by the specialist; the stated value then determines the amount of the loan. The movie emphasizes the quality of the carpet not only as a consumer good but also as capital mediating moments of hardship and deprivation.

III. THE ELEVENTH CARPET: THE SOUND OF THE CARPET[30]

The prominent Iranian director Abbas Kiarostami focuses on a Bijar carpet (Bijar is a town in North-West Iran), also called the Iron rugs of Persia or "the man's rugs" because of their durability and resistance to folding, made mostly by Kurdish and Afshar ethnics (and popular in the United States). The movie depicts a carpet both as an object and as an entry point to another form of cinematography that is the carpet itself. According to the Iranian film director Bahram Beyzai carpets are a precursor to cinema. In this short film, the camera moves over a carpet, between word and image, linking visible and performative elements through Iranian traditions of poetic conversation (*goft-e goo*). The film creates three episodes of a poetic conversation where the audience participates in hearing, seeing, feeling, remembering, recalling, and imagining as shifting voices move between and among subjects that are both absent and present. The voice-over nostalgically mimics a pre-revolutionary radio program that was extremely popular for its focus on traditional Iranian poetry and music called "*golhay-e rangarang*," or colorful flowers.

The first sequence is a female voice asking the spectator, à la connoisseur, "to open their eyes and see the manifestation of the lover all over." A shift to a male voice creates a new sequence as he reads the poem that is woven into the design of the carpet while the camera depicts the image of a cypress tree—repeated in the carpet design—which the poem addresses. The cypress tree is a singing tree in Iranian legends, a tree with the capacity to talk to humans. The poem continues by asking the cypress tree why it does not bear any fruit. The cypress tree's answer, as recited in the poem, is that "the free minded does not have any possessions."

The second sequence is back in the female voice as she recites a poem about lovers who sing a love song in their memory while stopping to talk to each other. This sequence moves beyond both the visual and the spoken word to appeal to memory, where one could converse with a lover without seeing or speaking.

The juxtaposition of poetry, image, voice, music, and the script woven into the carpet, as well as the cinematography of the carpet as it mobilizes subsequent scenes and pictures interrupt the pedagogy of the teleological and technical narrative of connoisseur books. While the film challenges Orientalist painting, and documentary films, and their investment in depicting the carpet as an exchange value, it eroticizes use-value as tactile, non-reproductive, and relational.

IV. THE FIFTEENTH CARPET: THE EMBODIED AUTHENTICITY OF IRANIAN-NESS

The Copy Cannot Beat the Original, directed by Mohammad Reza Honarmand, starts with an epigraph stating that "John Singer Sargent, the famous American painter, has said the collection of Italy's paintings during the Renaissance are not as valuable as a single Persian carpet. He is responsible for his words." Honarmand's film takes place in Kashan, at a home-based workshop where women are weaving and men are dyeing the yarn. (Most small- and medium-sized carpet-making workshops are located in traditional urban houses with many rooms situated around a courtyard). The film focuses on a conversation between a dealer and the owner of the carpet workshop. The dealer, who is involved in trade with China, tells Haji, the owner, how Chinese are making various kinds of hand-knotted Iranian carpets, including Kashan carpets, in large-scale production. The film juxtaposes the urban architecture of Kashan as a city when depicted through the gaze of the dealer who needs carpets that are produced faster and sold cheaper. The film ends with a comparison between German cars, owned by the dealer who believes no one can steal it, and Haji's claim about the impossibility of forging Iranian carpets. This film represents carpets along with traditional architecture as the embodied expression of Iranian-ness and impossible to replicate. Questions of fake versus authentic carpets are not limited to films, and some carpet-selling websites. For example, the costly effects of competition faced by Iranian families who depend on carpet-making for their income is articulated through a number of writings on the Persian carpet industry.

This film also exposes anxieties over the global competition between household-based and small- and medium-sized production. Carpets produced through the affective and collective cooperation between labor and capital are of higher quality than carpets made through large-scale production. The household operation is attached to a particular location, but capital needs to move freely in search of cheap labor in a global marketplace. Furthermore, cultural capital, including a carpet's design, which is rarely subjected to copyright rules and regulations, have become as mobile as labor and capital.

Affective Consumption

The filmic representation of Persian carpets constructs the nation in a number of ways: as gendered and ethnicized, as territorial and physical, aesthetic and sensual, as well as timeless and primordial. As I illustrated in this chapter, the transformation of Iran from a carpet nation to nation as a carpet involves two occurrences. The first one is the fetishization of Oriental and Persian carpets as encompassing a supernatural and magical force, a material thing with ambivalent immaterial power in their Orientalist portrayal. The second one involves

the nation coming to life through the carpet as its spirit. If in the first occur-
rence, the carpet is domesticated in order to fix the boundaries of the Oriental
and the Occidental, then in the second instance, the carpet as a mnemonic
commodity becomes the material evidence of the mythical time of the nation,
a time beyond reach, guaranteeing the futurity of the nation. In both instances,
the carpet's oscillation between an Orientalist and a nationalist temporality
makes the carpet a multifarious and hybrid product that crosses the boundaries
of subjects versus objects as well as distinct social orders and national borders.
However, what facilitates the commodifications of nation as a carpet is purchased through flows of affects.

I use the concept of affective consumption to refer to a communitarian act.
We are never alone when we consume something affectively. Connectivity is the
key word here. This emotional connection to the Others has been colonized by
an imperialist consumption of the Other. Also, affective consumption is central
in the production and reproduction of the nation as an imagined community.
The nation as commodity functions as a force that regulates groups affectively,
similar to how governmentality functions. Nations are not static and are not
only experienced textually but emotionally. Nations regroup and govern individuals, creating relations of affective solidarity. Functioning as a member of a
nation is already functioning within the structure of modern governmentality
and affective connectivity.

Furthermore, affects can function in two ways: as surpassing the threshold
of this connectivity and as a virtual co-presence of potentialities. In the case
of the Persian carpet, its potentiality is in its sensory aspect, as a product that
conceals and exposes the sensation of touch but also goes beyond it given that
vision is also mobilized in co-representing this form of potentiality. The carpet
is depicted as an eco-imaginary place or a paradise with the capacity to travel
in the sky, and in the clouds of imagination. With this ambiguous aesthetic,
an abstraction of the stories that take place in a village, the carpet is an early
computer in its capacity for networking, transporting information, and in its
potential for mobility. It is an old virtual object and a material object with the
ability to form and inform realities.

The nation as commodity continues to be symptomatic of a postcolonial
modernity that is producing a national or diasporic identity for the purpose of
political cohesion in the context of a neoliberal consumer culture.

Notes

1. Rassam Arabzadeh, *The Innovator of Persian Rugs*, compiled by Abbas Sarmadi (in
   Farsi with some English Translations) (Tehran: Yasssavoli Publications, 2003), 3. In
   a postmodernist move, a few carpet artists including pioneering Ostad Rasam Arabzadeh have transformed the carpet design by opening it up to innovative weaving,

design, and color. This includes his reversal of "*ghalat-bafi*/error weaving" or making mistakes while weaving the carpet to a style that is not rule-bound; cross-bordering the carpet frame; the unification of warm and cold, wild and domestic; and the replacement of color with image. See Arabzadeh, *Innovator of Persian Rugs.*

2. The Iranian railway started in the early twentieth century as part of the imperial railway project, which authorized the British citizen Baron Julius de Reuter to construct railways in Iran. However, the trans-Iranian railway was started again after the Reza Khan Coup d'état in 1921 and was completed in 1938. For more information, see Mikiya Koyagi, "The Vernacular Journey: Railway Travellers in Early Pahlavi Iran, 1925–50," *International Journal of Middle East Studies* 47 (2015): 745–763; Steen Andersen, "Building for the Shah: Market Entry, Political Reality and Risks on the Iranian Market, 1933–1939," *Enterprise and Society* 9 (2008): 1–33; S. John Galbraith, "British Policy on Railways in Persia, 1870–1900," *Middle Eastern Studies* 25 (1989): 480–505; J. Paul Luft, "The Persian Railway Syndicate and British Railway Policy in Iran," in *The Gulf in the Early Twentieth Century: Foreign Institutions and Local Responses,* ed. R. I. Lawless (Durham, NC: Center for Middle Eastern Studies, 1986), 158–215.

3. The 1919 agreement was designed by the British government and intended to turn Iran into the British protectorate. See, among others, Homa Katouzian, "The Campaign Against the Anglo-Iranian Agreement of 1919," *British Journal of Middle Eastern Studies* 25, no. 1 (May 1998).

4. Karl Marx, *Grundrisse, Foundations of the Critique of Political Economy* (London: Penguin Group, 1973[1939]), 494.

5. Leonard M. Helfgott, *Ties That Bind. A Social History of the Iranian Carpet* (Washington and London: Smithsonian Institution Press, 2001), 16, 278.

6. According to Helfgott "In the thirty-year period between 1873 and 1914, hand-knotted carpets evolved from luxury furnishings for the very wealthy to mass-produced" (Ibid., 15).

7. Persian-carpet connoisseur books link the history of the knotted carpets to the history of Persia, and even before the time of Cyrus the Great of the Achaemenid Empire (600–530 BC). See Fabio Formenton, *Oriental Rugs and Carpets* (London: The Hamlyn Publishing Group, 1972).

8. Indeed, the largest handwoven carpet in the world, at 60,546 square feet, was made for Abu Dhabi's Sheikh Zayed Mosque by Iranian weavers from Neishabour in Khorasan Razavi Province by 1,200 weavers for a period of one year and half and released in 2007. Read more: Hadley Keller, "The Incredible Story Behind the World's Largest Rug," www.architecturaldigest.com/story/worlds-largest-persian-rug-abu-dhabi-sheikh-zayed-mosque.

9. Helfgott, *Ties That Bind,* 15.

10. Martin Rudner, "The Modernization of Iran and the Development of the Persian Carpet Industry: The Neo-Classical Era in the Persian Carpet Industry, 1925–45," *Iranian Studies* 44: 54–55.

11. Rey Chow, *The Protestant Ethnic and the Spirit of Capitalism* (New York: Columbia University Press, 2002), 48.

12. With the modernization of patriarchy, middle-class women became educated housewives in need of learning and improving their skills, from creating and maintaining a respectable household to raising children to learning etiquette on how to behave. This process of housewifization required new consumer goods, from women's magazines to home furniture and appliances. Also, with the translation and publication of European and American home-economics books, a new consumer market targeting women was formed. See Pamela Karimi, *Domesticity and Consumer Culture in Iran* (New York: Routledge, 2013) for more examples. The "pedagogic state" in Afshin Marashi's terms, is one of the core components of nation-state formation, in *Nationalizing Iran: Culture, Power and the State, 1870–1940* (Seattle: University of Washington Press, 2008), 86.

13. Rudner, "The Modernization of Iran," 57.

14. Nitasha Kaul, "Cultural Econo-Mixes of the Bazaar," in *Postcolonial Economies*, eds. Jane Pollard, Cheryl McEwan, and Alex Hughes (London: Zed Books, 2011).

15. Kajri Jain, *Gods in the Bazaar: The Economics of Indian Calendar Art* (Durham, NC: Duke University Press, 2007), 78–82.

16. Shokooh Torkyan Velashani et al., "Effects of Physical Factors on the Sense of Security of the People in Isfahan's Traditional Bazaar," *Procedia. Social and Behavioral Sciences* 201 (2015): 168. Also, a number of bazaar buildings, including the Shiraz bazaar, were built in the late nineteenth and twentieth centuries. See Willem Floor, *Wall Paintings in Qajar Iran* (Santa Ana, CA: Mazda Publishers, 2005).

17. Rudner, "The Modernization of Iran."

18. Nestor Garcia Canclini, *Consumers and Citizens: Globalization and Multicultural Conflicts* (Minneapolis: University of Minnesota Press, 2001), 159.

19. Jila Rassam Arabzadeh was quoted by the paper as saying. http://mostaqueali.blogspot.com/2015/08/persian-carpets.html.

20. Many diasporic carpet traders and entrepreneurs are from Jewish or Armenian backgrounds. Both ethnic-religious groups have been involved in carpet trades both in Iran and the United States since the early twentieth century. Two large carpet stores in Los Angeles were established in beginning of the twentieth century. One of the stores is owned and named after an Iranian-Armenian trader and the other is owned by a Jewish businessman. Also, a number of Iranian antique dealers and carpet entrepreneurs in New York and Washington, DC, have Jewish backgrounds.

21. For more information, see www.incc.ir/en.

22. For an ethnographic study of Iranian Bazar, see Narges Erami, *The Soul of the Market: Knowledge, Authority and the Making of Expert Marchlands in the Persian Rug Bazar* (unpublished doctoral dissertation, New York: Columbia University, 2009).

23. Cited by Heynen and Baydar in *Negotiating Domesticity: Spatial Production of Gender in Modern Architecture* (London and New York: Routledge, 2005), 17.

24. The culture of domesticity included the act of consuming household commodities along with the gendered targeting of advertisements, both in print media as well as

radio and TV. Most recently, with the expansion of TV to the most remote parts of Iran, TV series produced in both Iran and Turkey are a site of household furniture and appliance consumerism.

25. As Freedgood states, "Layers and layers are needed to resolve the crisis of coziness, to address the problem of keeping inside spaces safe from the violence in the world outside that produces their furnishings." Elaine Freedgood, *The Ideas in Things: Fugitive Meaning in the Victorian Novel* (Chicago: The University of Chicago Press, 2006), 64–65.

26. From http://gabbeh.com/about_rugs.php.

27. In *Foundational Fictions* feminist scholar Doris Summer brilliantly illustrates the intimate relationship between modern heterosexuality and patriotism. See Doris Summer, *Foundational Fictions: The National Romances of Latin America* (Berkeley: University of California Press, 1991). A number of essays in Kaplan, Alarcon, and Moallem, eds., *Between Woman and Nation: Transnational Feminisms, and the State* (Durham, NC: Duke University Press, 1999) elaborate extensively on national narratives, gendered subject positions, and sexual desire.

28. This trend continues and even consolidated with the signing of a Bilateral Investment treaty between Iran and Japan in 2016.

29. The so-called Iranian school took center stage during the presidency of Mahmoud Ahmadinejad and the nomination of Esfandiar Rahim-Mashaie, a strong advocate of this tendency, whose nomination to be his first vice-president provoked controversy among the state elite.

30. In reference to "Is There a Place to Approach and Spread the Carpet?", a poem by Sohrab Sepehri, a prominent Iranian naturalist poet quoted in the film.

5

BETWEEN CARPETS AND COMPUTERS

Figure 5.1 **The Power Loom**
Photographed by Minoo Moallem

"Persian rug: a Paradise at your feet."
From (http://micheleroohani.com/blog/2010/02/03/
persian-rug-a-paradise-at-your-feet/)

As the carpet moves from Iran to various diasporic locations its representation takes new directions as a home far from home. New value is invested in the Persian carpet, as Iranian immigrants return to the more exotic notion of "Persia" and "Persians" to distance themselves from the politics of the Islamic Republic and Euro-American Iranophobia and Islamophobia.[1] Using carpets to return to a pre-Islamic notion of national identity and repossess the homeland makes Iranian ethnicity into a tangible and material everyday practice of doing identity. The symbolic value of belonging to the glorious time of the Persian Empire generates new desires to consume the carpet not only as a commodity but also as connection to the homeland.

In this context and with the expansion of new media and computer technologies, the carpet as a transnational commodity circulates beyond the conventional networks of trade via websites and ethnic TV. Through this recirculation, Persian carpets signify Iranian-ness as a transnational ethnicity, redefining and reinvesting new symbolic value in the carpet as a commodity.[2] The hybridity of the carpet both in terms of its design as well as its networks of trade makes it a privileged site of doing ethnicity for diasporic Iranians who are coming from various religious, cultural, political, and linguistic backgrounds.[3]

In this chapter I focus on two interconnected topics. First, I discuss the Persian carpets as a signifier of a diasporic ethnicity, elaborating further on the "net" and the "work" involved in the production, circulation, and consumption of rugs in cyberspace beyond Iranian territorial borders. Second, I delve further into the mediation of technologies of weaving and its disconnection from the modern invention of computers through two occurrences: the militarization of the carpet industry and its techniques of production, and the separation of weaving from the networks of knowledge and power. The affective assemblages involved in this process collapse carpets with monetary value into commodities with communal values disconnected from the history of labor. To elaborate further on this argument, I take up how the hegemonic power of the masculinist history of sciences has separated the history of carpets from the history of computers and foreclosed.

The subordination of women's modes of knowing and doing to the masculinist history of science and technology is indeed inseparable from the production of carpets as commodities that represent we-ness and otherness as both affectively desired and disavowed. As noted by Stiegler, the relationship between the human and the matter is the 'twin faces of the same phenomenon."[4] This process also relies on a technical imagination that detaches weaving as an embodied and sensory work from the carpet as a commodity, depicting a technoromantic landscape in its utopian (parasitical design) and dystopian (war carpets) form. This process conceals the perpetuation of feminized exploitative labor in the so called Oriental and Persian carpet industry and reveals the modern desire to conquer and domesticate nature through consumer culture. Possessing the carpets as a technoromantic landscape may be a shortcut to possessing what is desired and disavowed in modernity and postmodernity through a series of binary oppositions, the subject and object, culture and nature, mind and body, the Occident and Orient, the civilized and primitive, the male and the female, the home and the diaspora, labor and commodity, and the human and the machine.

In this context, the Deleuzian theory of assemblage/agencement and the spatialized notion of extension that I introduced as part of my methodological framework are helpful in thinking and writing about the connections between the net, the work, and the technologies of carpet weaving, including formations that stretch from culture to economy to bodies and technologies. It would be impossible to understand these formations without linking the carpet as a material thing with its image, text, and context. In the context of a global consumer society where the manufacturing of commodities, their circulation, and their consumption are scattered around the globe and in cyberspace, the configuration of how and in what ways these proximities and distances are regulated and governed through the flow of commodities is indispensable for our understanding of culture and economy. While I use the notion of extension as a methodological approach to explore the connection between the events that take place in diverse spaces, assemblage as a theoretical concept comprehends the compositional unity of bodies, objects, and machines (as existing things) as well as operative knowledge discourses (and concepts). The concept of assemblage grasps both ordering, reordering, and disordering while the concept of extension introduces the spatial dimension in the complex configuration of the carpet as a transnational commodity.

This chapter moves with the carpet to diasporic spaces as well as online homepages to illustrate how new meanings are invested in the carpet as it becomes a site of ethnicity further removed from the labor. Also, while the interplay of surface and depth in both carpets and computers as interfaces have a lot in common, the attachments and the assemblage work together to keep the commodity in circulation while locating both weavers and the technologies of weaving in the archaic and primordial time of tradition. In this context, the binary of tradition and modern is put into practice to distinguish between a distant world of fixed and unchanged traditions (sometimes depicted as a taste of Iran's glorious days of the Safavid empire and sometimes as the unchanging and primitive world of nomads and tribes) and technologies both desired and refuted by moderns. The magic of the Persian carpet as a civilizational commodity and a symbol of otherness, as well as its infinite existence as a national or ethnic commodity and a site of we-ness, remove human agency and manual and tactile labor from view. As I have shown in previous chapters, both the spectacle of commodity and the spectacle of labor are there to put the carpet on view as a unique commodity treasured only for display. Reconnecting carpets and computers in this chapter is a move away from the separation between the commodity, the labor, and the technology toward uncovering the convergence between productive labor and digital labor in their power to create, communicate, and transform.

Homeland Made in Diaspora

I met with Mr. Hekmat in his showroom in San Francisco on April 28, 2012. Mr. Hekmat is a fifth-generation modern carpet workshop owner from Azerbaijan.

We sat in his office, a large room with a beautiful Shiraz carpet, along with a nice desk and various issues of *Hali* magazine. I asked him why he thinks the carpet has become such a popular commodity. "It is very simple," he responded,

> carpets are the most instrumental of all objects. In primitive societies, they made their tents with carpets and they covered the floor with the carpet, they also used the carpet as a curtain to create different sections in the same tent. The carpet also functioned as a means of transport. People rolled their belongings in a carpet and moved around. The carpet is indeed the most utilitarian commodity.

Mr. Hekmat's juxtaposition of the carpet's use value and the carpet as a mobile commodity makes it either a must-have commodity or a piece of movable property. The origin story of the carpets as use value in his recounting makes the carpet an essential part of human history, from so-called primitive societies to modern ones.

Mr. Hekmat has a mobile and transnational operation. He has transferred his production mainly to India and Pakistan, with some in Turkey. He notes that the cost of labor in Iran is very high given that the weavers now ask to be paid on an hourly basis.[5] Furthermore, the US embargo against Persian carpets pressured many carpet dealers and traders to transfer their operations to other countries where they could monitor the production and circulation of the carpet. Mr. Talatie, a carpet entrepreneur who has a shop in Sydney, Australia, runs a similar operation. He takes the most popular carpet designs among his clients to the South of China to be made, and then sells his products in Australia. Similar to Mr. Hekmat and Mr. Talatie, Mr. Mehrzad owns one of the major carpet showrooms in LA and has a transnational operation. Mr. Mehrzad and his family have been in the carpet trade, especially export to the United States, since the 1950s. He is from a Jewish background and moved his business entirely out of Iran to LA after the Iranian revolution of 1979. He sells both antique as well as contemporary carpets. Mr. Mehrzad is very protective about his operation and how he imports the rugs to Los Angeles, but he did share with me that as a few other traders and sellers do, he exports the carpets first to Istanbul, Dubai, or Abu Dhabi and then to the United States.

I also interviewed Mr. Nabi, a Turkish trader, in June of 2012, in Istanbul to get a better sense of this system. He has a carpet store on the periphery of Istanbul's big bazaar. He calls his shop a hub for the circulation of all kinds of carpets, along with Persian rugs, to other parts of the world, including Europe and the United States. Mr. Nabi has no problem importing carpets from Iran to Turkey, and once they are in Turkey they are easily exported to the United States or Europe. The transnational operation of the carpet trade relies on global networks of labor, capital, and new media technologies to overcome national rules, restrictions, and regulations. When I asked Mr. Nabi about the US embargo, he smiled and responded, "As long as consumers want to buy a commodity, no state can prevent its trade." However, the restriction imposed by the United States on Persian carpets has had two consequences: it has facilitated the production of lower-quality carpets outside Iran and has made Persian carpets more expensive, given the multiple mediations involved in this process, without benefiting the weavers in Iran.

Given that almost 85 percent of Persian carpets were exported to the United States before the Iranian revolution of 1979, with the US embargo, the Iranian carpet industry went through new transformations. One significant consequence of the blockade has been the export of Persian carpets to other parts of the world. There has also been further fragmentation of carpet production, mediation, and consumption, including the creation of new circulating centers in Istanbul, Dubai, and Abu Dhabi, where carpets could be brought from Iran and sold to visitors outside the country. Consequently, there is an increasing overlap of the formal trade of Persian carpets with their informal exchange, facilitating a neoliberal order even though Iran has a relatively independent economy. Another effect is that Persian carpets are passed off as Turkish, Indian, or Afghani so they can enter the US market.[6] The embargo also shifted part of the carpet production toward new consumer subjects, diasporic Iranians who can go back and forth between Iran and various diasporic locations or simply purchase from carpet sellers outside Iran.

The US embargo thus made the affective consumption of carpets much more forceful, both for Iranians in Iran and Iranians in diaspora, since owning a Persian carpet means resisting the US embargo for Iranians in Iran, and a sign of Persian identity and Iranian ethnicity for the diasporic community transnationally.[7] With the recent removal of US sanctions vis-à-vis carpets in 2016, the situation has changed and exporting the carpet to the US has become popular again.[8] However, a conflict of interest is occurring between the Iranian carpet entrepreneurs who are making the carpet outside Iran and those who export carpets to the US from Iran. To distinguish the carpets produced externally from those made inside the country, the Iranian carpet industry is foregrounding questions of quality as well as the carpet as an extension of Iranian artistic talents, as I showed in Chapter 4.[9]

With transnationalism, mass migrations and the weakening of territorial nationalism, the notion of homeland has lost its sole attachment to a particular space. As a result, an economy of affects attaching specific commodities to the idea of the nation has found new currency. For transnational migrants, certain commodities create linkages between where they are coming from and where they live. Persian carpets have become this type of commodity. For diasporic communities, the home becomes an immigrant's private museum of symbolic meanings and remembrance. As noted by Firouzeh Mirrazavi, "An Iranian's home is bare and soulless without it, a reflection on the deep-rooted bond between the people and their national art."[10] Carpets as sensory products channel "sight" as they recreate what is familiar, homey, material, and sensual. In this context, carpets territorialize home and belonging. Also, as sensory commodities, rugs create space for the tactile memory of bodily touch, transforming the process through which carpets are produced in various parts of the world, including Iran, into a nostalgic sense of attachment to the nation.[11] For example, touching is crucial when buying a carpet both in terms of the feel of it and the distinction between a handmade carpet and a machine-made one.[12] Furthermore, given that shoes are mostly removed when one walks on the carpets, its aesthetics necessitate the sensory body. This form of attachment produces an affective response to the presence of a carpet, provoking the active participation of social subjects in this process.

More recently, the concept of home has migrated from a homeland or a territorial nation-state to computer "homes," "websites," and "homepages."[13] Virtual space has become a place to live, produce, and exchange what makes one feel at home, a place of comfort, a place of trade, a location of exchange, a place where belonging gets to be renewed through networks of information. Any space, cyber or real, is a site of ambiguity and in-between-ness for immigrants, where they never feel the comfort of the house, home, or homeland. As Ella Shohat argues, "The notion of original and stable home is thus cybernetically redefined for dispossessed nations not simply as a physical location but as a relational network of dialogic interactions."[14]

Most Iranian diasporic houses, like many other immigrant households, are both a manifestation of style as well as a site of exchange between the homeland and the diaspora. Ethnic commodities, including carpets, are bought and sold, not only by the inhabitants of the household but also by the members of family and friends who visit from Iran, to ensure the continuation of an affective community of the nation. The homeland becomes a mobile entity that feeds the visual needs of the immigrant communities to connect with what is lost—a sense of connectivity that is put in danger, open to forgetting, or to becoming something else. This resistance is not only an effort to protect tradition or the nation as such, but the sensual appeal of commodities in a consumerist global economy. Coziness and warmth, as I noted earlier, are two essential components of home as a domestic and domesticated territory, and this is experienced materially through patterns of everyday consumption. Feeling at home indeed refers to the commodities that surround immigrants at home, where they can collect and display what they like. Home becomes a site of memory, and the memory of home and homeland converge in transnational migrations where the idea of both of them blends through cultural practices of cooking, decoration, style, and color, maintaining a notion of collective identity as well as memory. The desire for the home and the homeland converges with the desire for the commodity, reconciling consumptive production with productive consumption.

As the carpet turns into a home far from home for Iranian diasporic communities, it has also become a signifier of middle-class culture in Iran. The desire for carpets in this case is oriented in three directions: the carpet as a site of Iranian ethnicity, the carpet as the signifier of national resistance against the US embargo and sanctions, and the carpet as the sign of class distinction and middle-class home décor. In all three cases, a new set of values is invested in the carpets as the consumer-subjects become further and further detached from sites of labor. This involves weavers as well, even in their embodied proximity to the loom, given that the culture of consumption has become an important part of everyday life; selling the hand-knotted carpets in order to purchase machine-made carpets has reoriented the weaving toward exchange value.

Selling and Buying the Nation Digitally

During my last visit to Talie Abad in 2015, when I was talking to a group of women weavers, one of them jokingly said: "I will only answer your questions if you take me to Los Angeles afterward." With the expansion of cable TV and the internet to the remote villages in Iran, the worlds of production and consumption have converged in new ways. Commodity fetishism is still using the concept of a home away from a homeland or a territorial nation-state to define commodities on a homepage. However, even though many weavers now have access to homepages and computer technologies, the networks of production, trade, and consumption are such that women in Talie Abad are not able to bypass these networks to sell their products online. Commodities mediated between the private and the public in colonial modernity, and now they continue to bring together "the empire of merchandise" in Roland Barthes' terms, with "the empire of the home" in Anne McClintock's terms.[15] As selling and buying have increasingly extended to new media spaces, they foster the blurring of public and private while strengthening the aesthetic and sensorial attachment to notions of them and us, as well as modern and traditional. For example, the concept of "traditional" on many carpet-selling websites turns the purchasing of the carpet into "the magical story that began thousands of years ago"[16] since Persian carpets[17] "represent ancient magical jewels."

Modernist notions of the private and the public are interrupted as the home and the market converge in virtual space. The internet becomes a place to live, produce, exchange, buy, and sell what makes one feel at home; it is a place of comfort, trade, and exchange, where belonging gets renewed through affective desires and needs. While Iran is not connected to the credit card system globally, cyberspace has become a primary site of selling and buying carpets for Iranian diasporic entrepreneurs. This situation, according to Amin, a rug entrepreneur located in Iran, has impacted the production of carpets in the country. According to Amin, what is sold as Persian carpets nowadays are mostly woven in China, India, and Pakistan using low-quality yarn, fewer knots, and low-quality dyes.

While some theorists have discussed the possibility of a fluid and ambiguous identity on websites and in cyberspace, carpet-selling websites, along with ethnic media auctions hosted on Iranian TV stations in Los Angeles, are still promoting transnational forms of nationalism through commodity circulation, claiming an identity that is primordial, static, and essentialized for consumerist purposes. The object of consumption comes to stand for this fixity and security of identity. That is why the carpet-selling websites are still heavily relying on the performance of modern Orientalism, nationalism, and ready-made notions of identity. That is to say, carpet-selling websites intervene in the economic, social, and cultural constructions of the Persian carpet. Indeed, a significant amount, if not all, of carpet-selling websites create a sense of identity that conceals both the experience of displacement and the transnational regulation of labor and capital. Instead, they create continuity between the past and the present by promoting the carpet as a commodity that animates "security" for unsettled and fluid identities in postmodernity.

In my close review of more than 50 Persian carpet-selling websites, most not only sell carpets but also provide services such as cleaning and repairing. These websites are sometimes linked to brief histories of Persian carpets without an option to buy or sell. Most of these websites are located outside Iran, and those inside Iran are mostly informational. All websites start by defining and explaining what is unique about Persian carpets. Some of them give a historical narrative, in the style of connoisseur books, in the "about us" section. The primary language is English (as opposed to the main language of carpet-selling ethnic TV channels, which is Farsi) targeting both Iranians and non-Iranians. However, the text of many of these websites is sentimental, constructing the carpet as the finest and most exquisite form of expression of Iranian-ness and boasting that the "best specimens available today rank amongst the highest level of art ever attained by mankind."[18]

For example, one website describes Persian carpets an ancient commodity:

To look at a Persian carpet is to gaze into a world of artistic magnificence nurtured for more than 2,500 years. The Iranians were among the first carpet weavers of the ancient civilizations and, through centuries of creativity and ingenuity building upon the talents of the past, achieved a unique degree of excellence.[19]

The text of most of these websites connects Iranian people to their art in an intrinsic and natural relationship. This serves as another account that essentializes carpet making as inherent to the Persians who do it. Many websites also urge diasporic Iranians to purchase the carpet not only for home decoration but as something that will emotionally connect them to Iranian art and culture. As stated by Mr. Shabahang "Authentic Persian carpets can be viewed as a reflection of the past and an expression of the Persian way of life."[20]

Questions of authenticity are central to many of these websites, which mostly define authenticity as being linked to a particular location in Iran and having been in business for a long time ago, sometimes starting in the late nineteenth century, before going online. Authenticity is also defined by the quality and durability of the Persian carpet. For example, excellent durability; not creating allergies or pollution; better cleaning and staying clean longer; absorbing and retaining better dyes; uniquely combining natural dyes for added artistic value; and not fading or deteriorating with age, like machine-made rugs and carpets do, are key features of the Persian carpets.[21]

The carpet is described as a commodity that creates a sense of connection to the imagined and affective community of the nation with a shared past and present. The nation as carpet becomes the commodity where the production and consumption of it either at home, in the homeland, or elsewhere in diaspora connect everyone to everyone else. In this context, the Persian carpet is represented as a commodity that makes it possible to think about affinity and affects in a transnational world. The carpet materializes the nation while also functioning as linking "us" and "them," and creates a sense of connection beyond time and space. For example, on the day in 1981 when 52 US hostages were released after 444 days of captivity in Iran, the Rezaian carpet company located in San Francisco received worldwide attention for offering each former captive a rug of their choosing worth $1,000. For years before and since, Rezaian has proudly proclaimed, "I'm Iranian by birth . . . American by choice."[22]

The language used in some of the web pages personifies carpets and even sexualizes them. For example, "Oriental rugs are one of the most sensual forms of fine art ever produced. Walk into any carpet showroom and see what I mean: suffused with rich color, elaborate design, and luxurious textures, the Oriental rug almost begs to be unrolled, stroked and admired."[23] Carpets are also represented as commodities in need of care. They need to be repaired, washed, and taken care of so they can become more and more beautiful. Many websites offer instructions for taking care of antique and luxury carpets. The ownership of luxury carpets is not only a sign of affluence but also synonymous with present day celebrity culture and the idea of success according to Mehraban's carpet selling website.[24]

Carpets are regularly auctioned in carpet-selling stores as well as on ethnic TV. My review of what I call "ethnic televised auctions" shows that most of them use cultural identity, Iranian art, and music to sell carpets. They call on the audience's culture of hospitality toward guests and appreciation for art and culture. Persian TV auctions are held a few times a week on various TV channels located in Washington, DC, Los Angeles, and other parts of the world, both in English and in Farsi. The English-language TV auctions mostly target non-Iranian collectors and consumers, whereas the Farsi TV auctions target diasporic consumers, mostly selling inexpensive carpets. Both Farsi- and English-language auctions rely on a connoisseurs' discourse to sell. Most auctions are mediated either by a white male or an Iranian salesman, not necessarily a carpet connoisseur. In these auctions, hand-knotted Persian carpets are distinguished from machine-made and handmade tufted rugs (a carpet made without tying knots, reducing labor time and the price) because of their quality, durability, and the density of the weave but also for the use of natural colors. Purchasing carpets is represented as a lifestyle rather than an act of consumption.

While there is some literature on the significance of eBay and cyber auctions, there is not much writing on the "ethnic cyberspace" and how enacting cultural identity through carpet consumption becomes a site of ethnicity. Some of the TV auctions not only sell carpets but also material objects that reinforce attachments to diasporic politics and the *ancien régime* by offering prizes, including coins from the Pahlavi era, to their audiences. Some of the newly designed carpets targeting diasporic consumers include signs, symbols, and icons from the pre-Islamic Persian empire.

As a consumerist interface, the world of homepages and ethnic auctions participate in the codification and separation of weaving, sensing, chatting, and knowing from the carpets as commodities, even though touching or tactual perception is crucial for interacting with the online information. This gap between manual work and commodity abstraction has defined both productive consumption and consumptive production since colonial modernity.

Weaving as Digital

On a visit to the Computer History Museum in Mountain View, I was shocked and surprised by the untold story of the carpets and computers. In the museum, the only instance where the history of carpets and the history of computers intersect is in the description of the Jacquard loom in 1801 as the first usage of stored data in commercial production and patterned code on large punch cards. The history of the linkages between weaving and computing as well as information on the influences of carpet weaving on computers is still to be written. However, what is consistent in this display is the construction of both women as "unskilled workers" and carpet looms and computers as technologies that enable unskilled workers, such as secretaries and weavers, to produce more efficiently. The Computer Museum display of the history of computers is among so many others that expose how modern spaces of museums are fitting artistic creativity and scientific innovation into the linear logic of a progress narrative. They also create space for the perpetuation of a Eurocentric knowledge.

The genealogy of the invention of the computer has been traced to "great men" of the Industrial Revolution, including Joseph Marie Jacquard, a silk weaver who created an enhanced textile loom in 1801. The Jacquard loom was the first machine to use punched cards to control the weaving of every single row of a patterned fabric, and it operated 25 times faster than the draw-loom. The extraction of "speed" in managing productivity went together with the development of masculinist and militaristic scientific inventions. The separation of the loom from the weavers, I argue, subordinated the rich culture of collaborative, artistic, and technical knowledge of rural and tribal female carpet weavers in the colonies to male technological inventions, expelling female weavers to the realm of the natural, tribal, and primitive.

Thus, it would be very difficult to talk about carpets and computers in the same frame of reference without interrogating two interconnected problems that have existed since colonial modernity. First is what I have discussed in previous chapters regarding the discourse of progress and the construction of Oriental carpets as belonging to the world of nature, magic, and tradition. This discourse provided justification for the mass production of Persian carpets under exploitative conditions. Second, as I also showed, during the period of national formation Persian carpets were invested with the characteristic of an authentic object belonging to the timeless essence of the nation. But this process suppressed the genealogy of carpets as modern commodities with layers of mediation and control in their production, circulation, and consumption.

Technological objects and artifacts inform us about how culture and technology converge and influence each other. They also expose the nature of continuity, connectivity, and change in technology as influenced by society. But, though objects are an important part of the history of technology, I have not come across any historians of science who consider the linkage between carpet looms, carpets, airplanes, and computers. Carpets and looms are represented as pre-modern, belonging to another temporality—the temporality of the primitive. However, as I argue, modern imagination and innovation are influenced by textiles and technologies of weaving.

The story or the history of science in the West has consistently been written from a Eurocentric and masculinist perspective. As I have shown in the prior chapters, the Eurocentric framework creates a dichotomy between the West and the rest, attributing science, progress, and development to the West while constructing the rest as having fallen behind since colonial modernity. The prevalent cultural racism vis-à-vis Muslim and Arab societies, including Iran, since colonial modernity has influenced the production, circulation, and consumption of Persian carpets as modern commodities.

So far, I have shown how knowledge and power intersect to produce and reproduce the world of Persian carpets as commodities belonging to an anterior time, in which either primitive weavers live, or a lost golden age of carpets can be traced back to, somewhere outside the temporality of the modern world of development and progress. The endurance of the carpets as commodities may be deconstructed through an interrogation of the history of masculinist science and technology. What is loaned out from the world of carpet weaving to the world of computers—including the language of patterns, webs and threads—tells a different story. As art historian Laura Marks argues:

> History is so deeply enfolded, so thickly interconnected, that it makes more sense to assume historical connections between things than to deny them. Apparent discontinuity, such as the division between the Islamic world and Europe, is actually enfolded history. As late medieval Europe constructed an autonomous and Christian identity, it disavowed its links to the Islamic World. Real historical ruptures, like ethnic cleansing of Spain in 1492 in which the state forced Jews and Muslims to either emigrate or convert, mark violent ends to intercultural exchange. Yet even in that example, Islamic (and Jewish) influence in European culture was not eliminated; it was just pushed underground.[25]

Indeed, creating a disconnection from Islamic history is a conscious epistemological and methodological strategy of a Eurocentric or Orientalist perspective that is at the core of an "imaginary geography," as Edward Said argues. Many scholars have argued that while historical connections between Islamic and European cultures have been obscured or belittled by earlier thinkers in the West, this is still influencing our ways of seeing, thinking, and speaking. Adding to this argument, as I go on to explain, this logic currently legitimizes militarism and neocolonial forms of war and occupation. Thus, we also need to interrogate the appeal of a militarized geography that justifies old and new forms of colonialism in the name of progress and development in everyday practices of consumerism. In this context, new forms of targeting based on transnational ethnicity and do-good consumerism participate in this process of militarization.

The Loom, the Computer, and the Body

Zahra is a master weaver. She is at once a poet, a spectator, and an actor. She is the one who defines the aesthetic experience of looking at the carpet; gazing at the carpet becomes an act of knowing, remembering, and experiencing the collective and interconnected sphere of experiencing life in the village. Zahra's articulation of her relation to the carpet rejects aesthetic experience as belonging to the world of the spectator and the spectacle for what exists beyond the world of "seeing," appearance, and self-consciousness. To see the carpet, one needs to rely on the realm of feeling, sensation, or desire and an embodied and collective experience involving the body, the loom, the home, and the market, calling for the recognition of a radical alterity independent of cognition. Carpet weaving as an event produces the carpet as a text through the crafting of the shapes, the colors, and the sounds. The carpet, in this case, is no more a commodity per se but an aesthetic experience.

(my field notes, August 2007)

Things happen when we start weaving a carpet. Women get sick; they die, they get into trouble in their relationships, they move to another location, all these events have an impact on the carpet. It is hard for the consumers of the carpet to identify this, but when I look at the knots in the back of the carpet, I remember all the

Figure 5.2 **The Body and the Loom**
Photographed by Minoo Moallem

events that took place during the weaving. The imperfection, the rupture, and the sadness are reflected in each knot. I can look at a carpet and tell you many stories and show you where it is reflected in the carpet.

(Soghra, from my field notes, July 2012)

Most weavers in the rural and urban areas cannot afford to use their own hand-made carpets; instead, cheap, mass-produced, machine-made carpets continue to populate the houses of rural and working-class people in Iran. However, the technology of the handmade carpet has remained exactly the same since the early eighteenth century. The machine-made carpet relies on the handmade carpet, and the handmade carpet relies on the antique carpet to keep the racialized bourgeois hierarchies of taste, race, class, and gender in place. Since museums have become "*des grands magasins,*" large department stores, in Baudrillard terms,[26] there is more of a convergence between art objects and everyday commodities such as carpets. However, while some art historians acknowledge the collaborative aspect of art work, the cooperative work of weavers continues to be disavowed.

Yet many of my interviewees in Talie Abad emphasize the collective aspect of the material and aesthetic creation of the carpet. While in high-profile museum exhibitions in the United States and Europe a return to arts and crafts has become a site of resistance for some feminist art historians and artists against the individualizing experience of high art, the representation of rural weavers as illiterate and lacking any cultural capital continue to proliferate. Rural and tribal weavers are mostly seen as filling a function in the chain of production. The designation of creative and artistic work to the space of high art and museums denies carpet weavers the ability to create symbolic capital. Because of that, the modern carpet industry has subjected the weavers of Persian carpets to this function; the rich tradition of collaboration and cooperation remains silenced and suppressed. This situation has created feelings of frustration for some weavers. Zahra mentions that most of the time middle-class women look down at her hands, with their traces of weaving, as rougher and tougher body parts that do not conform to normative notions of femininity. She feels ambivalent about her hands, "While I have a skill that can help me wherever I go, my hands are quite different from the hands of those who do not weave carpets."

The juxtaposition of the artistic, the technical, and the mathematical in the act of weaving creates webs of connections between the past and the present, the technical and the artistic, and the collective and the individual to bring the corporeal together with something that will live for an extended period. The carpet at the loom is a site of both visualization and virtuality, as it becomes a garden, a geometrical abstraction of shapes and symbols, a field of flowers and animals, or colors and shapes, or a paradisiacal view simulating the actual into the virtual. As Teshome H. Gabriel and Fabian Wagmister point out:

> Weaving is digital, in the sense that it relies on digits—on fingers—for its production. Digits, understood in this way, tend to emphasize the sensory, and more particularly, the tactile aspects both of technology and of culture per se. Thus, the digital involves a palpable relationality between producer, product, and culture. Digits imply a connection—a tactile, lived connection—to a wide array of cultural meanings, woven by the community as a whole, and handed from one generation to the next.[27]

For Gabriel and Wigmister, although there are vibrant and material connections between older ways of weaving and newer digital technologies, computer technologies have been constructed as radically different and disconnected from the past cultural and aesthetic traditions. In their view, terms such as "texture, pattern, layering, links, nodes, sampling, net, network, web, web weaver and threads belong to a lexicon employed in both weaving and computing."[28] Furthermore, computers use notions of interconnectedness and networking, and carpets do the same thing.

Bruno Latour and Antonin Lépinay, in discussing Gabriel Tard and his analysis of how modern science talks about the inventions of new machines, write: "A machine is an exterior talent, and a talent is an inner machine. Thus, the different and multiple skills of the craftsmen of old, their long apprenticeships and their gradual storing up of particular habits, all this was made mostly useless by the construction of later machines."[29] To understand the connection between carpets and computers, we should change our reliance on the definition of the machine and the commodity as separated from the knowledge and networks that create new inventions or innovations in tools. Weaving carpets is a fluid and flexible practice related to the lived experiences of many people and cultures around the world, from Africa to Latin America to Asia and Native communities in North America and other parts of the world. The commercialization of the carpets and their mass production as things Oriental or Persian since the late nineteenth century has disconnected the carpets from networks of memory about lived experiences, as well as multiple forms of encounters and crossings, aesthetically and technically.

The weaver's body is located near the loom. The loom functions as a computer screen, displaying the carpet while concealing the body. Such reticence precludes the panoptic intrusion of the industrial gaze as the weaver puts the design into action and shows the power to disarray and disorder. Thus, she becomes a source of both anxiety and desire. The representation of the carpet emphasizes the centrality of vision over embodiment. As Braidotti notes, "Embodiment means that we are situated subjects, capable of performing sets of (inter)actions which are—discontinuous in place and time."[30] Touch and sound become irrelevant to vision. To this embodied experience, touching and hearing are central. As Juhani Pallasmaa argues, "Sight is the sense of the solitary observer, whereas hearing creates a sense of connection and solidarity."[31]

Between Militarism and Consumerism

Consumer capitalism relies on militarism both in terms of technologies of production as well as the on-target militarized gaze of consumer culture. In the first case, as I argued in Chapter 3, the spectacle of labor turns weaving into a site of surveillance where labor is naturalized and exoticized as tribal, traditional, and primitive. Also, the construction of the technologies of weaving as disconnected from modern computing technologies have closed up the possibility of the carpet both as an interface and a surface connecting the commodity with laboring bodies. The enclosing of the carpet along with framing it as exchange value also suppresses what is left out in the realm of non-value. Furthermore, the invention of new technologies of weaving has been intimately related to the militarization of production in terms of speed and cost. This form of militarization is not only limited to representational practices and the spectacle of commodity or labor, as I discussed before, but it also includes material militarized tools to produce carpets in faster, less labor-intensive, and more cost-effective ways. Such examples include anything from the transformation of carpet looms to power looms, projectile looms, and Air Jet looms (shuttle-less looms using

Figure 5.3 **Tufting Gun**
Screenshot of a Tufting Gun

a jet of air to insert wefts and push the filling yarn), as well as tools such as the "tufting gun," which was developed in 1980 to produce handmade carpets without tying knots.

Second, the culture of militarism is using the language of carpets to target war and occupation, as in the example of carpet-bombing. As I noted in Chapter 2, carpet-bombing is the name that was given to the unguided aerial bombing that damages every part of an area, and has been frequently used by the United States since the occupation of Iraq and Afghanistan.[32] While consumerism has used militarism to target specific consumers, militarism is now using carpets to demarcate war, occupation, and destruction of specific landscapes.

The third dimension of this convergence of militarism and consumerism is the rise of war carpets. War carpets are hand-knotted carpets, and the newest version of what are called Oriental carpets.[33] They were originally produced in Afghanistan, though recently they have been made in other regions of the Middle East and South and Central Asia, including refugee camps in Pakistan. They are called by different names, including "conflict carpets," "crazy carpets,"

Figure 5.4 **The War Carpet**
Photographed by Minoo Moallem

Figure 5.5 **The War Carpet Segment**
Photographed by Minoo Moallem

and "terrorist carpets."[34] Yet all these names refer to carpets that are replacing images of nature, such as flowers, gardens, trees, clouds, etc., with images of modern weaponry, maps, tanks, rifles, grenades, helicopters, and other technologies of war as their key motifs. The carpet design reflects a fusion of modernist genres of art, including naturalism, with more vernacular colors and themes across the Middle East and South, East, and Central Asia.[35]

War carpets started after the occupation of Afghanistan and ended up aestheticizing war artillery. They are produced exclusively for the Western market. They began with the depiction of Soviet-made artillery from 1980 through 1989, but after the rise of the Taliban and the US occupation of Afghanistan, they began depicting other weapons and arms, including drones. According to Nigel Lendon, since 9/11, the depiction of the leaflets dropped on Afghanistan as US war propaganda has become an essential component of these carpets.[36] Currently, they are being vigorously exchanged over the internet (eBay and carpet websites), which includes a genre of design that is just called "war rugs." Not all war rugs depict artillery alone; some of them have maps of Afghanistan while others have figures of Afghan leaders.[37]

I suggest that war carpets maintain two contradictory notions. One is the suppression of the traumatic memory of war capitalism that cannot be recounted except as renewed or displaced forms of war and violence, but can be re-enacted in the spaces of consumerism. Sven Beker refers to mercantile capitalism as war capitalism to underline the centrality of the violence of slavery in the emergence and expansion of global capitalism.[38] However, war capitalism may not have ended or been completely replaced with industrial capitalism in the nineteenth century, but may have persisted in an altered state in neoliberal governmentality.[39] War carpets may be mending the crisis of meaning resulting from the contradictions and conflicts between the spaces of war and occupation in the Middle East and the spaces of everyday life in the West by creating an occasion where knowledge cannot be repressed. War carpets reveal how war is both indulged aesthetically and denied ethically. In my view, war carpets are a component of neoliberal assemblages in action, connecting the war zone to the imperial zones of everyday life.

War carpets depict the dystopian spaces of the current world where the landscape is occupied and destroyed by all kinds of weaponry. They are part of the militarization of space but also the military imagination of the world. They depict a de-territorialized hyper-reality linking the war zone of Afghanistan to collectors' and consumers' homes and the museum spaces of New York and Los Angeles. Indeed, if for collectors and museums in the United States, the war carpets are part of an old-fashioned virtual-reality entertainment world, in Afghanistan they are reminders of war and conflict from multiple occupations since 1980, by the Soviet Union and the United States, which have left devastating marks on people and landscapes. They are also a reflection of the harsh and exploitative conditions due to war and militarism under which the weavers (mostly women) are producing these carpets. In this context, the bodies on the ground are diminished as the images circulate.[40] What gets circulated both as commodities and as images are carpets depicting technologies of war, an aestheticized landscape bringing modern realism and naturalism together with militarism and consumerism to make an aesthetic claim.

The technoromantic landscape of military weaponry depicted in the war carpets may be able to make visible wartime conditions under which commodities are produced, circulated, and consumed. The contradictions between the fusion of the violent and the intended in this form of consumption are pressing for an interrogation of proximity and distance in the feminist politics of benevolence along with other humanitarian forms of consumerism.

In conclusion, the loom, the carpet, and the computer mediate a world of connections linking different operating systems while facilitating the regulation and control of information. The question is how best subjects/agents can interact with the information/pattern/design to challenge, revise, transform, or alter it. Both empire and nation function through webs of connections based on a decentralized, gendered regulation of labor both locally and globally. Within Iran, there has been a growing identification of the carpet as a site of national identity as well as national resistance to the US embargo, thanks to the expansion of the Iranian film industry and national television to the most remote areas in Iran. Furthermore, the consumption of machine-made carpets among rural and working classes in Iran has become a sign of class mobility. The carpet industry organizes itself on this interconnectivity and assemblage of various networks. Trade, production, circulation, and consumption are organized in a way that the work is performed continuously yet seldom regulated directly. The world of tradition is cut from the world of modernity and its temporality. In this context, the past becomes the prison-house of the present, not constitutive of it. The Persian carpets as material objects and sensual commodities fulfil consumer desires to enjoy what modernity is lacking in its break from the past and what the nation is yielding in the timelessness of a primordial identity. The evocation of these knowledge frames along with systems of production, circulation, and consumption keep the network of interconnections functioning through a security system that is sustained by various actors, including laborers.

The desire for community is continuously expressed through symbolic consumption. Carpets as a technoromantic landscape become a placeholder for what has been desired and disavowed since colonial modernity. It is through a series of binary oppositions—including the home and the diaspora, culture and nature, mind and body, the Occident and Orient, the civilized and primitive, the male and the female, and the human and the machine—that the versatility of labor is removed.

Notes

1. I define Islamophobia as a form of cultural racisms that is defined by two historical discourses: the discourse of race in its intersection with religion within the context of colonial modernity and the discourse of Xenophobia within the contemporary context of the United States and Europe. For a discussion of Islamophobia, see Junaid Rana, "The Story of Islamophobia," in *Souls* 9, no. 2 (2007).
   Iranophobia as a discourse mostly depicts the US and Israel's construction of Iran as a threat after the Iranian revolution of 1979 and the establishment of an Islamic Republic in Iran. For a comprehensive study of Iranophobia in Israel, see Haggai Ram, *Iranophobia: The Logic of an Israeli Obsession* (Stanford, CA: Stanford University Press, 2009).
2. As I have argued elsewhere, Iranian ethnicity is produced differently in various diasporic locations depending on the process of racialization in a specific location. See Minoo Moallem, "Transnationalism and Immigrant Entrepreneurship:

Iranian Diasporic Narratives from the US, France, England and Germany," in *The Social Construction of Diversity*, ed. Christiane Harzig and Danielle Juteau (New York: Berghahn Books, 2003) 104–127. However, Persian carpets mediate the materialization of an Iranian or Persian ethnicity that transcends the politics of race in a particular location.

3. Iranian diaspora constitutes Iranians who left Iran under different circumstances, including those coming from various religious and secular backgrounds (Jews, Armenian, Assyrian, Baha'i, Zoroastrian, Sunni, and Shia) as well as those from different ethnic backgrounds (including Kurds, Lures, Baluch, Turks, etc.) and political ideologies (monarchist, communist, Islamist, leftist, etc.). For more information on the Iranian diaspora in the United States and Europe, see Minoo Moallem, guest editor, special issue of *Comparative Studies South Asia, Africa and the Middle East*, on Iranian Immigrants, Exiles and Refugees XX, nos. 1 & 2; Minoo Moallem, "The Immigrant Experience: Affective and Effective Spheres and Issues of Race and Gender," *Soundings: A Journal of Politics and Culture* 11 (Spring 1999). See also Asgar Fathi, ed., *Iranian Refugees and Exiles Since Khomeini* (Costa Mesa, CA: Mazda Publishers, 1991).

4. Bernard Stiegler, *Technics and Time 1: The Fault of Epimetheus* (Stanford, CA: Stanford University Press, 1998), 178.

5. Questions regarding the transformation of labor laws in Iran especially after the establishment of the Islamic Republic vis-à-vis the carpet industry are very important. However, I have not studied these questions systematically in this work.

6. Moallem, "Transnationalism and Immigrant Entrepreneurship."

7. Even though the Iranian State has increased the non-oil exports, especially the Persian carpet, since the Iranian revolution of 1979, the US sanctions along with the cheaper cost of labor in China, India, and Pakistan have significantly impacted the Iranian carpet industry. According to Zahra Karimi "During 1994–2005 the share of carpets in non-oil exports has declined from 44.2 to 4.4 percent" ("The Effects of International Trade on Gender Inequality in Iran. The Case of Women Carpet Weavers," in Roksana Bahramitash and Hadi Salehi Esfahani (eds.), *Veiled Unemployment: Islamism and the Political Economy of Women's Employment in Iran* (Syracuse, NY: Syracuse University Press, 2011), 169. According to Eilland, in 1998, "India offers 65 percent of its carpets with Persian designs" (cited in Karimi, ibid., 179).

8. The situation may be changing under Trump administration, its Iranophobic agenda including imposing new sanctions and restrictions on Iran.

9. For examples, see recent issues of *Farsh Magazine (Nashrieh Farsh)*, which is published in Tehran, Iran (website: www.ircpe.com).

10. "Persian Carpet," compiled by, *Iran Review*, Tuesday, February 7, 2012. (www.iranreview.org/content/Documents/Persian_Carpet.htm).

11. Freudian notions of melancholy as unconscious mourning for a lost love is also relevant to this form of attachment, but this could perhaps be better understood as identity crisis. Lauren Berlant defines this form of attachment as identity crisis or even as a fantasy of the good life that is actually an obstacle to one's thriving as noted by Berlant. Lauren Berlant, *Cruel Optimism* (Durham, NC: Duke University Press, 2011), 1.

12. A smooth surface distinguishes a machine-made Persian carpet from a handmade one. Touching and pinching the carpet softly is necessary to identify a handmade carpet that resists the touch as opposed to being compressed like a machine-made carpet.

13. See Sima Shakhsari's work on Iranian Weblogistan and the significance of the internet for Iranian diasporic communities. See Sima Shakhsari, "Weblogistan Goes to War: Representational Practices, Gendered Soldiers and Neoliberal Entrepreneurship in Diaspora", in *Feminist Review* 99, 2011.

14. Ella Shohat, *On the Arab-Jew, Palestine, and Other Displacements: Selected Writings of Ella Shohat* (London: Pluto Press, 2017), 224.

15. Anne McClintock, *Imperial Leather: Race, Gender and Sexuality in the Colonial Contest.* (New York and London: Routledge, 1995), 18.

16. Alrug.com/Persian-rugs.html.

17. http//medium.com.

18. http://apersianrug.com/HIstory/history.html.

19. http://persia.org/Images/Persian_Carpet/carpet.html.

20. Anne Gilbert interview with Bahram Shabahang the co-owner of Orley & Shabahang Persian Carpet Gallery, in Antiques & Art Around Florida, 2009 (http://aarf.com/persiansf03.htm).

21. From the website: www.rugs-oriental.net/persian-rug-value.htmlQuality.

22. http://monarchinteriors.com/storewide_sale.htm. Carpets have been used as a site of diplomacy in other occasions. For example, Rassam Arabzadeh in his magnificent carpet "the Mirror of the Universe" includes a verse from a poem by the prominent Iranian thirteenth-century poet Sa'di Shirazi saying that "The sons of Adam are limbs of each other" emphasizing the oneness and the equality of all human beings as parts of a universal body in several languages (including French, English, Arabic, Chinese, etc.). Arabzadeh dedicated this carpet to the United Nations but his carpet was rejected because of its depiction of the geopolitical inequality between the Global North and the Global South causing death and destruction. See Rassam Arabzadeh, Innovator of Persian Rugs, Ibid, 122.

23. ww.bonhams.com/cgibin/public.sh/pubweb/publicSite.r?sContinent=USA&Screen=carpets2.

24. www.Mehraban.com/newsletter.

25. Laura Marks, *Enfoldment and Infinity: An Islamic Genealogy of New Media Art* (Cambridge, MA: The MIT Press, 2010), 26, 27.

26. Ludovic Leonelli, *La Séduction de Baudrillard* (Paris: École Nationale Des Beaux-arts, 2007), 84.

27. Teshome H. Gabriel and Fabian Wagmister, "Notes on Weavin' Digital: T(h)inkers at the Loom," *Social Identities* 3, no. 3 (1997): 354–355.

28. Ibid., 355.

29. Bruno Latour and Vincent Antonin Lépinay, *The Science of Passionate Interests: An Introduction to Gabriel Tarde's Economic Anthropology* (Chicago: Prickly Paradigm Press, 2009), 55.

30. Rosi Braidotti, "Cyberfeminism With a Difference," in *The Feminism and Visual Culture Reader*, ed. Amelia Jones (New York and London: Routledge, 2003), 532.

31. Juhani Pallasmaa, *The Eyes of the Skin: Architecture and the Senses* (England: John Wiley & Sons, 2005), 50.

32. Marc W. Herod, in his "A Dossier on Civilian Victims of United States' Aerial Bombing of Afghanistan," documents the Afghan civilian casualties of these bombardments (www.uscrusade.com/vic/). The concept of carpet-bombing has also been used in other contexts, including Susan Faludi's reference to the carpet-bombing of emancipated women in the 1980s. See *Backlash: The Undeclared War Against American Women* (New York: Broadway Books, 2006), X.

33. Some of these carpets are also made in Iran given the demand for these carpets and the concentration of a number of Afghani refugees in the carpet industry in Iran.

34. A number of sellers of war carpets challenge the notion of terrorist carpets. In their view, the emergence of these carpets goes back to 1979 and the reaction of Afghan people to the occupation of Afghanistan by the Soviets (www.rugrag.com/post/Afghan-War-Rugs-3dCultural-Artifacts—Terrorist-Rugs-3d-Ignorance.aspx).

35. Contrary to these carpets, in a critical move, Rassam Arabzadeh uses Cubism inspired by Picasso to weave a rug that is depicting the horror of war. He writes "I have tried to portray here some aspects of fighting, bloodshed, starvation, misery and poverty that are all associated with war. In my view, those who think of war as a way of achieving their aims are mad." Rassam Arabzadeh, *Knots of Love. A Collection of Fine Artistic Rugs by Master Rassam Arabzadeh* (Tehran: Tehran Naqsheh, 1371/1992), 39.

36. Nigel Lendon, "One Half of an Imaginary Conversation," April 25, 2017, in rugsofwar.wordpress.com.

37. See www.warrug.com/price.php for some examples.

38. Sven Beker, *Empire of Cotton. A Global History* (New York: Vintage Books, 2014).

39. I believe the Foucauldian concept of governmentality, as an ensemble of the practices of governments, technologies of power, and subjects made governable, best captures our neoliberal social context.

40. Foucault uses the concept of biopower to explain how modern nation-states invest in some lives while disinvesting in others. Agamben uses the two concepts of the state of exception and bare life to talk about those subjects that are denied both legal and political representation. See Foucault, *La Volonté de Savoir* (Paris: Gallimard, 1976), and *Society Must Be Defended* (New York: St. Martin's Press, 2003). See Giorgio Agamben, *Homo Sacer: Sovereign Power and Bare Life* (Stanford, CA: Stanford University Press, 1998).

EPILOGUE

In an essay entitled "The Metaphor of the Eye," Roland Barthes, referring to Georges Bataille's *Histoire de L'oeil*, asks the question, "How can an object have a story?"[1] In this book, I have told the story of the Persian carpet as a commodity, from the aestheticization of the Persian carpet as part of Orientalia to its transnational circulation from one location to another.

Through various chapters of this book, I tracked the relationship between the image and the commodity, not limiting it to commodity fetishism but as a relation that produces sociality at all levels.[2] As I demonstrated here, as the Persian carpet moves in time and space, it gains new symbolic value. So, the story of the Persian carpet is a transnational story linking a heterogeneous assemblage of material objects, social subjects, meaning systems, and images since colonial modernity. It registers multiple encounters culturally and aesthetically along with a myriad of border crossings. While carpets are classified, categorized, and branded as unique to specific regions, nations, and localities, the carpet design is perhaps the most enduring representation of a hybrid assembly of symbols and signs, as well as texts and textures, from various cultures from Central and South Asia to East and West Asia (or the Middle East).[3]

The trajectory of Persian carpets from their genealogical advent as a sign of pure otherness to their nationalization and ethnicization as a sign of identity is marked by the transnational convergence of labor, capital, and systems of representation. Throughout this book, I demonstrated how crucial it is to go beyond modern dichotomies—including economy and culture, subjects and objects, work and non-work—to access the multiple folds in the story of the carpet.

Informal imperialism's control and management of the flow of Persian carpets from luxury objects to mass-produced commodities in the late nineteenth century was instrumental in facilitating the movement of raw materials and chemical dyes from Britain to sites of carpet production in Iran. However, it also enabled consumptive output in the aftermath of the establishment of a modern nation-state in Iran. Carpets gradually became a national commodity displaying Iranian identity as material, tangible, and substantive. After the Iranian revolution of 1979 and the establishment of an Islamic Republic; various immigration waves of Iranians, mainly to the United States and Europe; and the US embargo on Persian carpets, the carpet was reconfigured both as a site of national resistance as well as a signifier of ethnic identity, causing a counterflow.

As a vital matter, the carpet is indeed more than its modern genealogy as an object separated from subjects or as a cultural artifact isolated from the natural environment. The carpet is perhaps the oldest remainder of cultural *métissage* and cultural hybridity, as its design traces multiple forms of crossings. That is why as the carrier of an excess, carpets were prone to the ideological invasion of modernity and its construction of Orientalia as evoking authentic otherness. In other words, carpets are not only remnants of a moment of closure in capitalist commodity circulation and its regimes of ownership, identity, and security in the transnational context of trade and commerce, but they are also material objects that provoke other forms of cultural desires and pleasures.

The carpet is perhaps one of the oldest things that has endured the separation of the body from the work, the process from the product, the textile from the text, and the semiotic from the symbolic. Predominantly performed by women, weaving is one of the oldest forms of creative labor to visualize and textualize events that have taken place in time and space. Hence, women's authorship has been tamed, disguised, and reoriented toward the modern desire for the carpet as a commodity. Retrieving the abject in the carpet by recognizing the meaning of creative labor as itself a relationship to modern imperial and national patriarchal modes of signification may be a way to reassemble what is gradually lost at the juncture of commodity, capital, and representational practices.

Notes

1. Roland Barthes, "The Metaphor of the Eye," *Critical Essays,* translated from French by Richard Howard (Evanston, IL: Northwestern University Press, 1972), 239.
2. This includes meaning making and the very psychic formation of gendered subjectivity, according to some feminist scholars. In her reading of Julia Kristeva and Lacan, Kathryn Sullivan Kruger links weaving and female textual production, calling this process a *thetic* threshold between the text and the textile, the abjectification of the maternal body and the author's desire to recover and recoup this body within the symbolic order. In her view, "The weaver's desire to articulate autonomy as well as to seek (re)union outside of the self (remember, autonomy conditioned by a sense of loss and desire for the [M]other) produces a textile which is itself like a veil, another covering, beneath which the maternal body is concealed but never completely revealed." Kathryn Sullivan Kruger, *Weaving the Word: The Metaphorics of Weaving and Female Textual Production* (Cranbury, NJ: Associated University Presses, 2001), 37–38.
3. Some scholars have started to use the concept of West Asia and West-Asian to move away from the colonial concept of the Middle East. As noted by Joanna Kadi, the Middle East is"an appropriate name only if one is a colonizer standing West and invading East." Joanna Kadi (ed.), *Food for Our Grandmothers : Writings by Arab-American and Arab-Canadian Feminists* (New York: South End Press, 1994), XV.

INDEX

Page numbers in italics indicate figures on the corresponding pages.

Made in the USA
Monee, IL
22 December 2021